UNFORGETTABLE PACIFIC NORTHWEST CAMPING VACATIONS

UNFORGETTABLE PACIFIC NORTHWEST CAMPING VACATIONS

By KiKi Canniff

Ki² Enterprises
P.O. Box 186
Willamina, OR 97396

Library of Congress Cataloging-in-Publication Data

Canniff, KiKi
Unforgettable Pacific Northwest Camping Vacations / by KiKi Canniff.
        p.   cm.
    Includes index.
    ISBN 0-941361-06-3 $10.95
    1. Camp sites, facilities, etc. – Pacific States – Guidebooks.
    2. Pacific States – Guidebooks.   I. Title.
GV191.42.P16C36   1994
647.94795'09 – dc20
                                                        94-18169
                                                        CIP

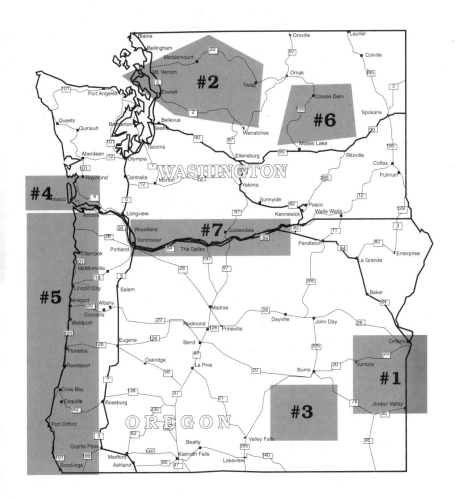

UNFORGETTABLE PACIFIC NORTHWEST CAMPING VACATIONS

Vacation #1 – **A Stark & Startling Adventure in Leslie Gulch**

Vacation #2 – **Magnificent Journeys along the Cascade Loop**

Vacation #3 – **High Mountain Trekking in the Steens**

Vacation #4 – **Kites, Sunken Ships, Old Forts, and a Drive on the World's Longest Beach**

Vacation #5 – **Picturesque Encounters at the Oregon Coast**

Vacation #6 – **An Ice Age Vacation in Eastern Washington**

Vacation #7 – **The Best of the Columbia River Gorge**

TABLE OF CONTENTS

INTRODUCTION

Anyone who has spent much time camping in America's northwest corner will tell you that there's no other place quite like it. This region's diverse landscape and rugged beauty is breathtaking.

Although the wild environment revered by its Native Americans has been forever erased in many locales, a significant number of wildly beautiful places still exist. Volcanic eruptions, ice age glaciers, prehistoric lakes, and erosion have all played a part in creating this unique landscape.

Choosing the best Pacific Northwest camping areas wasn't easy. Having spent most of my adult life exploring and writing about the two states, I've camped in plenty of one-of-a-kind places. In this book I've tried to include a variety of adventures. It was my goal to show each of you at least one new area, no matter what type of camping experience you prefer.

I'm an avid explorer, so for me there's nothing quite like waking up surrounded by nature. The sounds, the smells, and the sense of adventure are exhilarating.

My perfect campsite has a trail for exploring, and the possibility of seeing wildlife. At day's end I'm content to stare forever into the hypnotic glow of a campfire or to forego the warmth and gaze upward into a night sky untouched by artificial light.

Whenever the stresses of civilization get me down, I picture myself hiking over the crest of a hill. The air is crisp and pine-scented. Pausing to catch my breath, I drink in the primitive beauty of a lone campsite. A creek rushes by a few hundred feet beyond the tent, the sun sparkling on its water, and a red tailed hawk circles overhead.

Having stayed in more than 500 Pacific Northwest campgrounds, I've pitched my tent in plenty of places that look just like that vision. I've also spent the night in everything from barren desert camps to crowded lakeside RV parks. But somehow, this is the image that comes to mind when I think of camping in Oregon and Washington.

For campers, the fact that this two-state region has more than 2,000 public campgrounds makes it easy to enjoy the land. These vary from primitive near-wilderness sites to luxurious RV parks with all the trappings of modern civilization.

Whether your image of the perfect campground includes sleeping under the stars within view of a crystal-clear mountain lake, or sitting in your RV watching cable tv, the Pacific Northwest has lots of campgrounds just right for you.

As a rule, campers will find that the most luxurious campgrounds are privately operated. Some include swimming pools, hot tubs, saunas, game rooms, and laundry facilities as well as hookups for water, electricity, sewer and cable tv. The rates for two people range from less than $5 to more than $30 a night, depending on the location and amenities offered.

The vacations outlined in this book will provide a variety of camping experiences. However, keep in mind that even those places offering only primitive campgrounds are easily accessible from more civilized areas, and vice versa.

To insure that everyone will be able to find a campsite, the campgrounds listed in this book are all large and easily accessible. If you want a smaller campground, or one off the beaten path, check the listings in **Free Campgrounds of Washington & Oregon** and **A Camper's Guide to Oregon & Washington**.

Leslie Gulch, in eastern Oregon, is the most primitive and unique area included. Its remarkable landscape is the result of violent volcanic eruptions that have been shaped by 15 million years of natural erosion. The land is relatively untouched by mankind and should only be visited by those who intend to keep it that way.

On the other hand, northern Washington's Cascade Loop is just as accessible to travelers driving RVs as those in automobiles. Whether you have time to tour the entire 400-mile length or only a short stretch, you'll find plenty of campgrounds from which to choose. Traveling the loop is an excellent way to experience the mountains and forests that have brought people to the Pacific Northwest for hundreds of years.

Steens Mountain will give you the opportunity to enjoy the high desert country. Clear mountain lakes, spectacular glacier-carved gorges, wild mustangs, and Oregon's highest road are just a few of the attractions found here. Historic sites, plentiful wildlife, lava beds, and the Great Basin are all part of a vacation in the Steens Mountains.

A visit to America's northwest corner isn't complete without a look at the Pacific Ocean. Both states offer gorgeous coastal scenery. You'll find flat sandy beaches, agate-strewn coves, mountains that touch the sea, bustling tourist towns, quiet fishing villages, civil war forts, wilderness beaches, old growth forests, and lots of public land.

The area southeast of eastern Washington's Coulee Dam is also a great place to spend your vacation. The mighty Columbia River and beautiful Roosevelt Lake make it popular with water enthusiasts. Unusual geological sites like Dry Falls, a 3.5 mile wide Ice Age waterfall, and Steamboat Rock are another great reason to visit this area.

The Columbia River Gorge separates a particularly beautiful portion of Oregon and Washington. This region has been designated a National Scenic Area and contains numerous waterfalls, a great expanse of relatively undeveloped forest land, lots of hiking trails, and plenty of easily accessible scenic vistas. River traffic includes working tug boats, grain barges, refurbished sternwheelers, fishing boats, pleasure craft, and windsurfers.

Whether your next Pacific Northwest camping trip is a weekend outing or a two week vacation, I'm sure you'll find a destination in this book that will help you to make it unforgettable!

Happy camping,

KiKi Canniff

Camping Vacation #1

A Stark and Startling Adventure in Leslie Gulch

FROM THE AUTHOR'S JOURNAL . . .

I had covered a lot of miles that day, so it was late by the time I got to the Leslie Gulch turnoff. I knew the roads there were unimproved, and was anxious to reach my destination early, in case I was forced to turn back. I had no problem with the roads; what slowed me up was the totally awesome landscape.

Although I'd seen pictures of Leslie Gulch, I found myself completely unprepared, and mesmerized by the stark beauty and rich colors. This is Oregon's most dramatic landscape, and one that is completely different from any other Pacific Northwest setting.

I've always been in awe of the beauty in America's northwest corner, but arriving in Leslie Gulch I felt like a beggar at a banquet. The colors changed with the angle of the sun, and when night fell, it was with an all-encompassing darkness.

Leslie Gulch is not for everyone, for it is without the civilized touches that most expect. I hope that it will always be a pristine, time-sculpted environment whose only visitors are those who respect nature and leave no trace of their stay.

When I left, it was with a deeper respect for mankind's relatively short life span in relation to that of the earth.

Notes from my first Leslie Gulch vacation

A STARK AND STARTLING ADVENTURE IN LESLIE GULCH

Once you visit Leslie Gulch, it will remain forever in your mind as the Pacific Northwest's most unusual landscape. Located near Oregon's eastern border, it's a place of exceptional beauty. Relatively few people visit this treasure, for it is the rare vacationer who is willing to make the long journey across the state's dry southeastern desert.

Those who cross this arid land will find themselves in a magnificent setting. The gulch is lined with brilliantly colored rock spires that have been sculpted

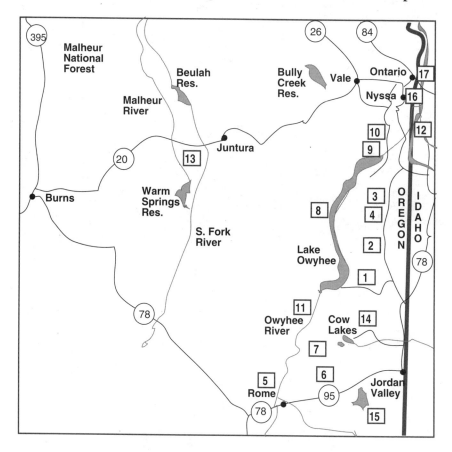

Leslie Gulch Area Attractions

by 15 million years of erosion. Together, the wind, water and time have created a starkly majestic landscape.

Even the region's title is steeped in color. This area was named for a turn-of-the-century cattleman, Hiram Leslie, who was struck by lightening in the gulch in 1882. According to local legend, Leslie had been accused of cattle rustling and, in defending himself, invoked the Lord to strike him dead if he was lying about his innocence. That very afternoon a lightening bolt knocked him from his horse. After lingering for a few days, he died.

Colorful Leslie Gulch

Leslie Gulch [1] can be reached from either Jordan Valley or Ontario. From Jordan Valley, take Highway 95 north 18 miles to where you will see a sign pointing west toward Leslie Gulch Road. This is the southern route, and will take you through steep-walled canyons, past towering rock spires, columns and pinnacles.

The best time of day to tour the gulch is early morning. When the first rays of sun make their way over the rocks, the range of colors and textures are astounding. Morning is also when you're most likely to see bighorn sheep, pronghorn antelope, mule deer, coyotes, wild horses, and lots of birds.

Sundown brings exotic colors to the sandstone and volcanic rock formations, and an eerie stillness to the surroundings. When night falls, it brings total darkness, and the sky is brilliantly clear. This is a great place for star gazing.

The Leslie Gulch region has been designated an area of critical environmental concern because of its unique vegetation, outstanding scenery and wildlife. Three wilderness areas, Upper Leslie Gulch, Honeycombs and Slocum Creek, have been established to protect the rare plant species.

There are only a few campsites within Leslie Gulch, and all are primitive. Campers, however, will find plenty of overnight accommodations in and near Ontario, Vale and Nyssa.

Leslie Gulch-Succor Creek Byway [2]

If you're coming from Ontario, you'll find the northern Leslie Gulch entrance near Succor Creek State Park, 40 miles south of town. This road is part of the BLM's National Back Country Byway System. Known as the Leslie Gulch-Succor Creek Byway, this 53-mile route is made up of gravel and dirt roads, with elevations ranging from 2,500 to 4,800 feet.

Succor Creek Canyon [3] is where the region's oldest rock formations can be found. It's also a great place to hunt for picture rock, petrified wood and thundereggs. The creek was at one time an important watering hole for early pioneers. It winds through an impressive rock canyon. You'll find primitive campsites at **Succor Creek State Park [4]** as well as restrooms, picnic facilities and hiking trails.

The byway is not suitable for travel when snowy or wet, and portions are best traveled in a high-clearance vehicle. However, much of the route is accessible to passenger cars as long as you drive carefully. The best time of year to travel the byway is May to October. The road is not recommended for RVs and trailers.

There is no drinking water available along the Leslie Gulch-Succor Creek Byway, so be sure you take plenty of water with you. Before traveling the byway it is also wise to contact the BLM office in Vale for current road conditions.

The Pillars of Rome [5]

Be sure to allow enough time during your vacation in the Leslie Gulch area to see some of the region's other outstanding attractions. No one should miss the Pillars of Rome, or the wild and scenic Owyhee River.

You'll find the Pillars of Rome north of Highway 95, about 20 miles southwest of Jordan Valley. On the way, you can take short side trips to see an extinct volcano crater and the grave of Sacajawea's son.

The Pillars of Rome are an intriguing collection of erosion-carved rocks that have taken on the images of castles and mountain fortresses. Although this, too, is an eroded landscape, it is not at all like that of Leslie

Gulch. The rock carvings tower high above a flat desert, like deserted ships on a calm sea. These delicately colored natural rock structures are on private property, so please be respectful, stay on the road, and enjoy this splendor only from your car.

History buffs will want to take the three-mile road to **John Baptist Charbonneau's Grave [6]**. Charbonneau was born to Sacajawea as she guided the Lewis and Clark Expedition westward. The turnoff is marked by a small sign, 12 miles west of Jordon Valley. Besides the gravesite, this area holds the rock ruins of Fortified House, Ruby Ranch, and a small ghost town.

Near milepost 12, on Highway 95, you'll see a gravel road leading north. This will take you through the sagebrush-dotted desert to an extinct volcano known as both **Jordan and Coffee Pot Crater [7]**. It's not visible from the highway, and is about a 20-mile drive. The volcano erupted 3,000 to 4,000 years ago and includes a number of smaller spatter cones. The lava flow covers a 30-mile area.

The surrounding landscape is riddled with lava tunnels. Visitors need to exercise extreme caution; it's easy to get hurt on the abrasive lava. Some of those hollow tubes are quite deep, so be careful or you could accidentally fall in, and it's hard to get out alone. There are no facilities at Jordan Crater.

Where to Cool Off
While in the Ontario area, you may wish to allow time to explore Succor Creek itself, swim in beautiful Lake Owyhee, go fishing, soak in a hot spring, or hunt for thundereggs. If you time your visit right, you can also attend the annual Obon Festival or Thunderegg Days.

Owyhee Lake [8] is Oregon's longest lake. Massive rock formations surround the water, creating a haven for trophy size bass. There are also plenty of campsites here, with both a state park and seasonal resort.

The dam, located at the northeast end of the reservoir, is 417 feet high. It's quite spectacular during spring run-off when the overflow cascades wildly into **Glory Hole [9]**. **Snively Hot Springs [10]**, along the Owyhee State Park Road, is also a pleasant treat.

Oregon's **Owyhee River [11]** cuts through a deep, steep-walled canyon that is filled with archeological sites. Some date back 12,000 years.

Floating the Owyhee is the best way to explore this area, but because many parts of the river have rock falls and wild water, it's not for novices. Rapids range from Class I to VI.

The river's 120 miles between Owyhee Reservoir and the Oregon/Idaho border are part of the National Wild and Scenic Rivers System. For a detailed boating guide to this area contact the BLM's Vale office.

Where to Fish
Anglers will find several lakes, as well as the Owyhee, **Snake [12]** and **Malheur Rivers [13]**, worth a visit. Owyhee Lake offers three concrete boat ramps and is stocked with crappie, bass and catfish. **Cow Lakes [14]**, northwest of Jordan Valley, also has a concrete boat ramp, crappie and bass.

Antelope Reservoir [15], southwest of Jordan Valley, has a gravel boat ramp and a good supply of trout. Catfish weighing over 30 pounds have been caught in the Snake River near Ontario. The Snake also has good crappie, bass and trout fishing.

Rockhounding and Annual Events
Rockhounding is a popular activity around here. The Succor Creek area is where you'll find thundereggs, Leslie Gulch Canyon has moss agates and jasper, and Jordan Valley offers agates and petrified wood. Other locales have obsidian, thundereggs, petrified wood, leaf prints, plume agate, jasper, and picture rock.

Every year, beginning on the second Wednesday in July, the town of Nyssa hosts a five-day event known as **Thunderegg Days [16]**. This is a good family festival with lots of special activities. One of the most popular activities are the organized tours to local digs where you can learn the art of rockhounding.

During Thunderegg Days you can also tour an extensive rock collection, compliments of the Treasure Valley Rock and Gem Club. Visitors also have the opportunity to purchase thundereggs, garnets, opals, fire agates, picture jasper, petrified wood and other rocks, as well as rockhounding tools and equipment.

Another charming local event is Ontario's annual **Obon Festival [17]**. Generally held the third Saturday in July, it has been observed here for nearly 50 years.

Obon is a special Buddhist observance that includes song, dance and traditional Japanese food. In Ontario, it's also a time when Buddhists and non-Buddhists join together for odori dancing to the rhythm of enormous taiko drums. The celebration is based on the legend of Moggallana, a high disciple of Buddha, who after saving his mother celebrated with friends.

Treasure Valley Buddhists have expanded this observance into a celebration of the Japanese culture. Tours of the temple, a variety of Japanese and American foods, authentic Japanese dancing, and other entertainment are included. This festival offers an excellent opportunity to learn about another culture and its traditions.

Whether your idea of a great vacation includes the pulsating drums of the Obon Festival or you're just looking for the quiet solitude of Leslie Gulch Canyon, this area will provide you with an unforgettable experience.

For Additional Information
Call the following agencies as soon as you decide to visit the Leslie Gulch area. Tell them what your interests are and when you are coming. They can provide detailed maps and information that will help you to make your vacation even more unforgettable.

Ontario Visitors'/Convention Bureau... (503) 889-8012

Nyssa Chamber of Commerce .... (503) 372-3091

Vale Chamber of Commerce .... (503) 473-3800

Obon Festival .... (503) 889-8691

BLM – Vale Office .... (503) 473-3144

Oregon State Parks .... (800) 452-5687

   (If calling from Portland .... 731-3411)

Leslie Gulch Area Campgrounds

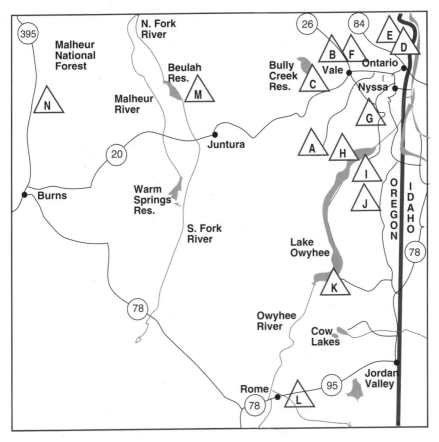

A) TWIN SPRINGS BLM CAMPGROUND
4 units – no fee, drinking water, vault toilet.

Take Highway 20 west of Ontario 3.5 miles and turn south onto Dry Creek Road. After 2 miles the road will become gravel. Stay to the left and follow it 24.5 miles to the campground.

B) PROSPECTOR TRAVEL TRAILER PARK
34 campsites – most w/full hookups – $15.00/night, tent area – $5.00/person, showers, laundry, ice, trailer waste disposal. Call (503) 473-3879 for reservation information.

Located in Vale. Take US Highway 26 north of its junction with Highway 20, and after 3 blocks turn onto Hope Street. The park is 1 block east.

C) BULLY CREEK RESERVOIR
66 campsites – most have electricity, showers, trailer waste disposal, swimming, fishing, boat launch, $6.00 to 8.00/night – $36.00 to $50.00/week. For reservations call (503) 473-2969. Located 9 miles west of Vale via Graham Blvd.

D) IDLE WHEELS VILLAGE
6 campsites w/full hookups – $13.00/night, no tents, showers, laundry, trailer waste disposal. For reservations call (503) 889-8433.

Located in Ontario, at 198 SE 5th Street.

E) COUNTRY CAMPGROUNDS
15 campsites w/full hookups – $10.00/night, plus some tent sites – $7.00/night, showers, laundry, trailer waste disposal, picnic area, hiking, fishing. Call (503) 889-6042 for reservation information.

Located 2 miles west of the Ontario airport, at 660 Sugar Avenue.

F) WESTERNER RV PARK
15 campsites w/full hookups – $10.00/night, some sites include cable tv hookups, tents okay, showers, laundry, trailer waste disposal, river, fishing. For information call (503) 473-3947.

Located in Vale, at the junction of Highways 20 and 26.

G) SNIVELY HOT SPRINGS BLM CAMP
Primitive campsite clearing – no fee, no drinking water, 136° hot spring.

From Nyssa, take Highway 201 south 3 miles and turn onto the road to Owyhee State Park. This primitive campground is 1 mile south of the Lower Owyhee Watchable Wildlife Site, about 12 miles north of the reservoir.

H) LAKE OWYHEE RESORT
61 campsites w/water & electricity – $9.00/night, trailers to 35', tents okay, lake, swimming, fishing, boat launch, boat rental, tackle shop & groceries. For reservations call (503) 339-2444.

Head south out of Vale on the road to Lake Owyhee State Park for approximately 38 miles. Also accessible from Ontario & Nyssa.

I) LAKE OWYHEE STATE PARK
40 campsites – 10 w/electricity – $13.00 to $14.00/night, trailers to 55', picnic area, showers, trailer waste disposal, boat launch, fishing.

Located about 33 miles southwest of Nyssa. Follow the signs to Lake Owyhee State Park.

J) SUCCOR CREEK STATE PARK
19 primitive sites – $9.00/night, no drinking water, hiking, picnic area, wildlife viewing site, rockhounding.

Located 30 miles south of Nyssa. Follow Highway 201 to the Succor Creek State Recreation Area Road; the campground is 16.5 miles from this point.

K) SLOCUM CREEK BLM CAMPGROUND
Primitive camping – no fee, no drinking water, picnic tables, boating, swimming, boat ramp, in Leslie Gulch, on Owyhee River.

Take Highway 95 north of Jordan Valley 18 miles and go left at the Leslie Gulch turnoff. After about 10 miles you'll reach Leslie Gulch Road; follow it about 15 miles to the campground.

L) ROME BLM CAMPGROUND
6 primitive units – no fee, drinking water, river, boat ramp.

Located at Rome, next to the Owyhee River.

M) CHUKAR BLM PARK
18 units, trailers okay, no hookups, drinking water, on Beulah Reservoir, hiking, $3/night.

From Juntura, head west on Highway 20 to Beulah Reservoir Road then north 6 miles to campground.

N) IDLEWILD FS CAMP
24 units, trailers to 32', no hookups, drinking water, picnic area, in Malheur NF, no fee.

Located on Highway 395, 17 miles north of Burns.

Camping Vacation #2

Magnificent Journeys Along the Cascade Loop

FROM THE AUTHOR'S JOURNAL . . .

Every time I tour the Cascade Loop, I am amazed at how close it comes to that picture-perfect image non-residents speak of when fantasizing about a Pacific Northwest vacation.

Towering snow-capped mountains, lush-green forests, wildly rushing rivers, pristine lakes, wildflower-filled mountain meadows and unbelievably gorgeous natural areas are all found along the loop. Looking closely, I catch glimpses of the natural grandeur once seen throughout the Pacific Northwest. I can't help but think to myself, see it now, before all of the old growth trees are gone: for even the newer forests are being leveled at a stomach-wrenching rate.

Each Cascade Loop town seems to have its own character, a quiet blend of the cultures that settled the region, and the industries that fueled it. It's a pity so many people whiz through these towns without sampling their specialties.

I will have to come back again soon, for this time my visit was much to brief. I must return to Leavenworth in the fall during one of their colorful Bavarian festivals, spend more time hiking along the western shores of Lake Chelan and in the mountains of the North Cascades National Park, and I really should rent a boat again and visit more of the smaller San Juan Islands.

Notes from a tour of the Cascade Loop

Photo courtesy of the Cascade Loop Association

MAGNIFICENT JOURNEYS ALONG THE CASCADE LOOP

When you drive Washington's Cascade Loop, you follow one of the most spectacular circular routes in America.

This 400-mile drive will take you through vast forests, beside sparkling rivers, into the shadow of snow-capped mountains, past crystal-clear blue-green lakes, into a number of intriguing small towns, and right by lots of great places to camp.

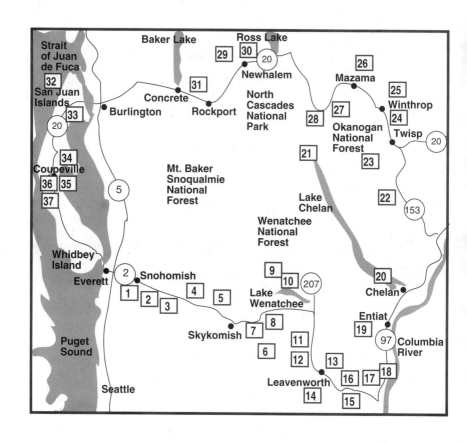

Cascade Loop Attractions

There's so much to see along the loop, that you could split the drive into two vacations and still miss spectacular sights. This route crosses the Cascade Mountains twice, meanders alongside several wild and scenic rivers, takes you into three national forests, and to one of America's most scenic national parks.

Getting on the Cascade Loop

The journey begins near Everett; take Highway 2 east of I-5. A stop in **Snohomish [1]** will give you a chance to shop in the region's greatest collection of antique stores. There are nearly 100 within a four-block area. This turn-of-the-century town has a vintage red-brick downtown area, several historic churches, and lots of elegant old wooden-frame houses.

Traveling east, you'll see the **Skykomish River [2]** along the highway's south side. This river is popular with canoeists, kayakers, and trout fishermen.

The state **salmon hatchery [3]** at Startup is a great place to learn about northwest fish. Visitors can walk among the man-made ponds and see salmon ranging in size from tiny fingerlings to mature adults.

Wallace Falls State Park [4], 2 miles northeast of Gold Bar, is the site of a thunderous 250' waterfall. If you follow the 2.5-mile trail to the falls you'll find a panoramic view of the luscious Skykomish Valley.

Continuing on Highway 2, you soon enter the **Mt. Baker-Snoqualmie National Forest [5]**. The Cascade Mountains have been here for over 15 million years, but this magnificent alpine landscape was created by glaciers within the last 500,000 years.

The Mt. Baker-Snoqualmie National Forest has an office in Skykomish where you can get maps and information. A stop there will enhance your enjoyment of the forest's 1.7 million acres. They can help you find wild rivers, hidden waterfalls, high mountain lakes, year-round glaciers, luscious alpine meadows, and 1400 miles of trails. Backpackers will want to ask about the **Alpine Lakes Wilderness Area [6]**.

Exploring the Stevens Pass Area

As the highway climbs Stevens Pass, you'll see the ferns, mosses and deep woods that typify a mountain rain forest. A good place for a close-up look is **Deception Falls [7]**, just east of Skykomish. A short trail there will lead you through the woods to where the waterfall cascades down the mountainside.

The view from 4,601-foot **Stevens Pass [8]** is expansive. Lofty Mount Index can be seen from one side, the beautiful Skykomish River from the other. The original forest is now gone, but the 6-foot diameter stumps found among the younger trees show the enormous difference between new and old-growth trees.

Stevens Pass has lots of hiking trails. You'll find them along both sides of the road, marked by turnouts and signs. At the summit you can see North America's longest railroad tunnel. It is 7 miles long.

Just beyond Stevens Pass you enter the **Wenatchee National Forest [9]**. Extending 135 miles along the eastern side of the Cascade Mountains, it includes 2.2 million acres and some outstanding recreational lakes. The forest provides 2600 miles of trails through high alpine country and sagebrush-dotted lowlands. The district offices at Lake Wenatchee and Leavenworth are excellent places to get assistance in finding the right trails for your level of endurance.

The **Lake Wenatchee [10]** turnoff is 20 miles east of Stevens Pass. This pristine 7-mile-long lake offers boat launches, swimming beaches, picnic areas, hiking trails, and campgrounds.

Continuing southeast on Highway 2, you'll soon spot the **Wenatchee River [11]**. It has lots of rapids, waterfalls, and is surrounded by a rugged landscape. The highway has lots of overlooks and trails, which provide easy access to this spectacular terrain.

As the river flows through **Tumwater Canyon [12]**, just west of Leavenworth, the water turns wild. This is a beautiful spot year round, but it's particularly gorgeous in the fall, when the trees change colors.

Bavarian Shops and Pioneer Log Cabins
Downtown **Leavenworth [13]** has been recreated to resemble a Bavarian-style village. It is filled with old-

world-style architecture, lots of flowers, specialty shops and German restaurants. If you follow **Icicle River Road [14]** out of Leavenworth, you can watch rock climbers scale the steep mountains. They come from all over the world to test their skills on these sheer granite cliffs. If you have a good pair of binoculars you can follow individual climbers all the way to the top.

Continuing on Highway 2, stop in Cashmere for a tour of the **Aplets & Cotlets candy kitchen [15]**. Tours are given June to December, on weekdays between 8:00 a.m. and 5:00 p.m., except during the noon hour, and 10:00 a.m. to 4:00 p.m. most weekends.

Cashmere also has one of the nation's finest collections of pioneer log cabins. Located at the east end of the Cottage Avenue Bridge, the **Chelan County Museum [16]** is open April to October. Hours are 10:00 a.m. to 4:30 p.m. Monday thru Saturday, and 12:30 p.m. to 4:30 p.m. on Sundays.

The cabins have been furnished to depict frontier life in the 1800s. Buildings include a one-room school, post office, barber shop, general store, assay office, millinery shop, jail, doctor's office, saloon, blacksmith shop, mission, railroad depot, print shop, and homestead cabins. Admission is by donation.

Highway 97 to Lake Chelan
Just past Cashmere the Cascade Loop takes you north on Highway 97. This is where you'll find the magnificent **Ohme Gardens [17]**. The work one family, they took several decades to create and offer a terrific view of the Wenatchee and Columbia River Valleys. The gardens are open daily, April to October, from

9:00 a.m. to dusk. The charge is $5.00 for adults, and $3.00 for children 7 thru 17.

At **Rocky Reach Dam [18]**, just north of here, you can take a free tour that begins with a hands-on exhibit explaining hydro-electricity. Other displays cover the Columbia River from prehistoric times to the present, early Indian life, and the huge paddlewheel boats that traveled these rivers in the late 1800s.

Continuing north on Highway 97, anglers may want to take a side-trip up the **Entiat River [19]**. The fishing is good, and there are several campgrounds.

The next loop highlight is spectacular **Lake Chelan [20]**. If you don't take the boat tour, you'll miss out on a rare treat. This gorgeous 55-mile-long lake ends in the **Lake Chelan National Recreation Area [21]**.

Photo courtesy of the Cascade Loop Association

Crystal-clear Lake Chelan sits in a glacier trough that measures over 8,500 feet from valley crest to lake bottom. Much of the surrounding land is accessible only by boat. You'll find a wealth of hiking trails leading to high mountain lakes, year round glaciers, panoramic vistas, hidden waterfalls and pools.

Two passenger ferries operate between the town of Chelan and the head of the lake. The *Lady of the Lake* runs daily, May thru October. Departing at 8:30 a.m., it stops in Stehekin for 1.5 hours, getting back to Chelan by 6:00 p.m. The cost is $21.00 round trip, $10.50 for children 6 to 11, and kids under 6 are free.

The *Lady Express* makes a faster journey. It operates weekends only from mid-May to mid-June, then daily until the end of September. It also leaves at 8:30 a.m., but is back at Chelan by 2:00 p.m. and only stops for an hour in Stehekin. The cost is $39.00, and kids 2 through 10 go for half price. Prepaid reservations are available on the *Lady Express*, call (509) 682-4584. You don't have to return the same day, and can go up the lake on one boat and return on the other.

The Methow Valley and an Old West Town
Continuing on the Cascade Loop, you take Highway 153 into the **Methow Valley [22]**. You'll find this road about 20 miles north of Chelan. It's a peaceful route that follows the Methow River through a wide basin.

The **Okanogan National Forest [23]** is west of the river. This is one of America's oldest national forests; most of its 1.5 million acres were set aside in 1897. The forest provides lots of hiking trails and camp sites. Stop at the ranger station in Twisp for personalized help in deciding where to go.

Heading northwest on Highway 20, you'll soon arrive in **Winthrop [24]**. This quaint little town recaptures the spirit of the old west. Its main street is lined with false-front buildings, wooden sidewalks, old-fashioned street lights, hitching posts, and watering troughs. Winthrop has the look of an 1890's mining town. You expect a stage to race through town at any moment.

A visit to Winthrop's 1897 **Waring Castle [25]** will teach you a lot about life here prior to the 20th century. This little museum is packed with pioneer memorabilia, Indian artifacts, antique printing equipment, horse-drawn vehicles, and even a few early automobiles. Situated on a hill behind town, the grounds provide a lovely view of the area.

The museum is open daily from 9:00 a.m. to 8:00 p.m. during the summer. The balance of the year it is open weekends only, from 10:00 a.m. to 5:00 p.m.

Mountain Pass Overlooks

Heading west along Highway 20, you begin the drive back over the Cascade Mountains. The scenery is gorgeous, yet looks quite different from the southern portion of this loop drive. Dozens of scenic overlooks and hiking trails can be visited along the way.

Washington, Harts and Rainy Pass are three especially scenic viewpoints. The road to **Harts Pass [26]** is 12 miles west of Winthrop, near the Early Winters Forest Service Information Center. Follow it 20 miles northwest for a spectacular view. This road is not recommended for trailers.

West of Mazama, about 16 miles, is where you'll find the **Washington Pass Overlook [27]**. It's only .5 mile off the highway. At the end of this paved road you'll find plenty of parking, and a wheelchair-accessible trail.

The view looks out over Early Winters Creek, and is dominated by Liberty Bell Mountain. This 5,477-foot-high overlook is surrounded by massive granite cliffs and snow capped mountains.

Rainy Pass [28] is just west of the Washington Pass overlook road, and where the Pacific Crest Trail crosses the highway. This 2,600-mile trail follows the Cascade Mountain Range from Canada to Mexico. Take the 1-mile paved overlook trail for a great view of the mountains and valleys around Rainy Pass.

North Cascades National Park

Leaving Rainy Pass, the highway takes you downhill 30 miles to Ross Lake. This portion of your drive leads you through parts of the Okanogan National Forest

Photo courtesy of the Cascade Loop Association

and into the **North Cascades National Park [29]**. The grandeur and beauty of this mountainous region is unforgettable.

Your travels will take you right past **Ross, Diablo and Gorge Lakes [30]**. All three are beautiful. You'll see the luscious blue-green waters of Ross and Diablo to the north, as you start down the hill. There are plenty of scenic overlooks where you can safely pull out of traffic to enjoy the view.

Between June 1st and Labor Day you can take a 4-hour excursion that includes a boat cruise on Lake Diablo, a tour of the Ross Dam powerhouse, and a ride up Sourdough Mountain on one of America's last incline railways. Reservations are required. Call Seattle City Light at (206) 684-3030 for details.

In 1968, North Cascades National Park was created to protect this region's wild alpine environment from further development. The 700,000-acre park has beautiful glaciated canyons, towering granite peaks, crystal clear lakes and year-round glaciers.

The park lands have very few roads, but lots of hiking trails. A number of trailheads are found along the North Cascades Highway, as well as Cascade River Road southeast of Marblemount.

If you intend to camp in the back-country, stop at any of the park's ranger stations for directions and a permit. There's no cost for this permit, but it helps the rangers to disperse visitors to avoid overuse. The visitors' center at Newhalem is another good place to get hiking information and permits.

You'll find the 1500-acre **Skagit River Bald Eagle Sanctuary [31]** between Marblemount and Concrete. There are several highway turn-outs near the primary viewing areas, making it easy to safely watch this symbolic American bird. If you look in the tops of the trees along the river, you'll have a good chance of seeing some of these magnificent birds.

The San Juan Islands
Continuing west on Highway 20, you are nearing the end of the Cascade Loop, and the beautiful **San Juan Islands [32]**. You can drive right onto two of the islands, Fidalgo and Whidbey. A bridge over Cornet Bay, at Deception Pass, connects the two.

From **Deception Pass State Park [33]** you have a spectacular view that includes several of the smaller islands within the San Juan Archipelago. Some of these are wildlife refuges and parks, but you need a boat to reach them. Camping and water sports, including scuba diving, are popular at the Deception Pass park.

Whidbey Island provides a pastoral setting and is where you'll find several important historic sites. The town of **Coupeville [34]** is filled with authentic false-front buildings. You'll also find an 1855 blockhouse, 1852 log cabin, some turn-of-the-century churches and lots of houses built between 1854 and 1899. The entire town is listed on the National Register of Historic Places.

At the **Island County Historical Museum [35]**, in Coupeville, you can learn about the area's history and pick up a self-guided tour map. The map will show you where you'll find Whidbey Island's most important historic sites, including the **Ebey's Landing National Historic Reserve [36]** and old Fort Casey.

Fort Casey [37] was built in the late 1890s, and currently serves as a state park. Facilities include an informative interpretive center, a few campsites and an underwater reserve.

To complete the Cascade Loop, take the ferry from the southeast tip of Whidbey Island to the mainland town of Everett. It's a short trip, and the ferry runs every 30 minutes. The view from the water is beautiful, and in the late spring and early winter you can hear sea lions barking.

Whether you have three days or three weeks, a vacation along the Cascade Loop is an adventure you won't want to miss.

For Additional Information
If you plan on visiting this area, call the Cascade Loop Association and ask for their free 64-page color brochure. It's packed with photos, maps and all kinds of helpful information. Hikers should also contact any national forest or park they intend to explore.

Cascade Loop Association .... (509) 662-3888

North Cascades National Park Service *and*
Mt. Baker-Snoqualmie Nat. Forest ..... (206) 856-5700

Wenatchee National Forest .... (509) 662-4335

Okanogan National Forest .... (509) 826-3275

Washington State Parks .... (206) 753-2027

Washington State Ferries .... (206) 464-6400

Cascade Loop Campgrounds

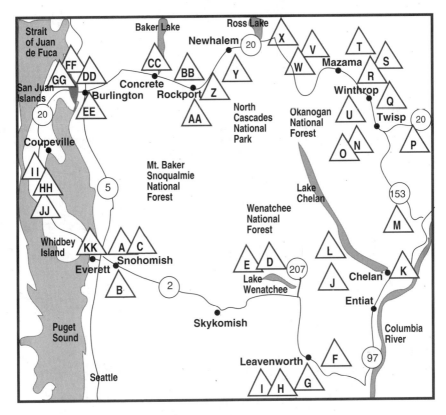

A) FLOWING LAKE COUNTY PARK

28 RV sites w/full hookups, plus 10 tent sites, flush toilets, picnic area, boat launch, swimming, fishing, pets okay, $10 to $14/night.

In Snohomish. Turn left off US 2 at milepost #10, drive 5 miles to 48th Avenue and turn right. The park is at the end of the road.

B) MONEY CREEK FS CAMP

24 units, trailers to 22', group sites, pit toilets, wheelchair accessible, picnic area, well, swimming, fishing, in Mt. Baker-Snoqualmie NF, pets okay, $10/night.

Take US 2 west of Skykomish 2.5 miles, then FSR 6400 southeast .1 mile to camp.

C) BECKLER RIVER FS CAMP

27 units, trailers to 22', pit toilets, fire pits, picnic area, well, fishing, swimming, in Mt. Baker-Snoqualmie NF, pets okay, $10/night.

Drive east of Skykomish 1 mile on US 2, then take FSR 65 north 2 miles to the campground.

D) NASON CREEK FS CAMP
73 units, trailers to 32', piped water, flush toilets, river, fishing, trail, in Wenatchee NF, pets okay, $8/night.

Northeast of US 2/State 207 junction. Take State 207 northeast 3.4 miles to CR 290, campground is west .1 mile.

E) LAKE WENATCHEE STATE PARK
197 units - no hookups, picnic shelter, wheelchair access, trailer waste disposal, summer programs, boat launch, fishing, swimming, pets okay, $10 to $11/night.

North of US 2/State 207 junction 6 miles on State 207.

F) TUMWATER FS CAMP
81 units, trailers to 20', no hookups, picnic area, handicap access, stream, flush toilets, fishing, hiking, in Wenatchee NF, pets okay, $8/night.

Northwest of Leavenworth 9.9 miles on US 2.

G) ICICLE RIVER RANCH
64 campsites, 52 w/full hookups, plus 12 tent sites, reservation information - (509)548-5420, showers, spa, putting green, river, swimming, fishing, $16 to 23/night.

Southwest of Leavenworth. Leave US 2 .5 mile southwest of town on Icicle Road. Campground is 3 miles.

H) EIGHTMILE FS CAMP
45 units, trailers to 28', handicap access, well, stream, fishing, hiking, in Wenatchee NF, $8/night.

Southwest of Leavenworth. Leave US 2 .5 mile southwest of town on Icicle Road. Campground is 8 miles.

I) JOHNNY CREEK FS CAMP
65 units, trailers to 28', well, handicap access, fishing, hiking, in Wenatchee NF, $7 to $8/night.

Southwest of Leavenworth. Leave US 2 .5 mile southwest of town on Icicle Road. Campground is 12.4 miles.

J) SILVER FALLS FS CAMP
35 units, trailers to 22', picnic area, well, stream, waterfall, fishing, hiking, in Wenatchee NF, pets okay, $5/night.

Northwest of Entiat. Leave US 97 1.4 miles southwest of town on Entiat Valley Road. Campground is 30.4 miles northwest.

K) CITY OF CHELAN LAKESHORE RV PARK
160 units, 151 w/full hookups, plus 9 w/water & electricity – tents okay, no dogs in summer, information - (509)682-5031,

reservations by mail only, showers, playground, trailer waste disposal, on Lake Chelan, swimming, fishing, bumper & paddle boats, go carts, mini golf, $13 to $22/night.

In Chelan, right on State 150.

L) LAKE CHELAN STATE PARK
146 units, 17 w/full hookups, reservations available in summer – (509)687-3710, wheelchair access, picnic shelter, on Lake Chelan, snack bar, trailer waste disposal, boat launch, scuba diving area, fishing, swimming, water skiing, $10 to $16/night.

Leave Chelan heading west on the road leading around the south side of Lake Chelan. Campground is 9 miles.

M) ALTA LAKE STATE PARK
1981 units, 31 w/water & electricity, community kitchen, wheelchair access, trailer waste disposal, fishing, swimming, trail, $10 to $15/night.

Take US 97 northeast of Chelan 17 miles, then State 153 west 2 miles to campground road, and follow south 2 miles to park.

N) POPLAR FLAT FS CAMP
16 units, trailers to 22', pit toilets, picnic area, piped water, river, wheelchair access, fishing, hiking, in Okanogan NF, $5/night.

Leave Twisp on CR 9114 and head west 10.8 miles, then take FSR 44 northwest 9.4 miles.

O) BLACK PINE LAKE FS CAMP
23 units, trailers to 22', pit toilets, picnic area, piped water, lake - no motors, wheelchair access, boat launch, boating, fishing, hiking, in Okanogan NF, pets okay, $6/night.

Leave Twisp on CR 9114 and head west 11 miles, then take FSR 43 south 8 miles.

P) RIVER BEND RV PARK
104 campsites, 69 w/full hookups, plus 35 tent sites, information - (509)997-3500, showers, laundry, rec hall, playfield, playground, trailer waste disposal, fishing, $13 to $17/night.

Southeast of Twisp 6 miles on State 20.

Q) METHOW RIVER/WINTHROP KOA
120 campsites, 16 w/full hookups, 52 w/water & electricity, plus 52 tent units, reservations - (509)996-2258, showers, laundry, groceries, trailer waste disposal, heated swimming pool, river, fishing, playground, $16 to $20/night.

Southeast of Winthrop 1 mile on State 20.

R) PEARRYGIN LAKE STATE PARK
84 units, 30 w/full hookups, 27 w/water only, reservations taken in summer – (509)996-2370, wheelchair access, trailer waste disposal, boat launch, fishing, $10 to $16/night.

At Winthrop, take Riverside north .5 mile, Bluff Street east 2 miles, and follow Pearrygin Lake Road to campground.

S) DERRY'S RESORT ON PEARRYGIN LAKE
154 campsites, 64 w/full hookups, plus 90 tent units, reservations - (509)996-2322, showers, laundry, groceries, playfield, playground, trailer waste disposal, on Pearrygin Lake, swimming, fishing, boat launch, $12 to $15/night.

Leave Winthrop on Riverside and go north .5 mile to Bluff Street, then east 2 miles to Pearrygin Lake Road. Camp is east 1 mile.

T) FLAT FS CAMP
12 units, trailers to 18', pit toilets, stream, wheelchair access, fishing, in Okanogan NF, no garbage service, pets okay, no fee.

Head north of Winthrop 6.6 miles on CR 1213, 2.8 miles on FSR 51, and northwest 2 miles on FSR 5130 to camp.

U) BIG TWIN LAKE CAMPGROUND
86 units, 20 w/full hookups, 26 w/water & electricity, 40 w/out hookups, plus tenting area, information - (509)996-2650, pull-thrus, showers, laundry, trailer waste disposal, playground, lake swimming, boat rentals, fishing, $11 to $15/night.

Take State 20 south of Winthrop 3 miles, then follow Twin Lake Road west 2.3 miles to campground.

V) KLIPCHUCK FS CAMP
46 units, trailers to 32", stream, flush & pit toilets, wheelchair access, fishing, hiking, in Okanogan NF, $6/night.

Head northwest of Mazama 4 miles on State 20, and take FSR 300 northwest 1.2 miles to camp.

W) LONE FIR FS CAMP
27 units, trailers to 22', piped & well water, pit toilets, creek, wheelchair access, fishing, view of Silver Star Glacier, in Okanogan NF, $6/night.

Northwest of Mazama 11 miles on State 20.

X) COLONIAL CREEK NCNP CAMP
164 campsites, trailers to 22', no hookups, information - (206)856-5700, wheelchair access, flush toilets, well water, picnic area, summer program, trailer waste disposal, at Diablo Lake, fishing, boat launch, hiking, in North Cascades National Park, pets okay, $10/night.

About 1.5 miles south of the Diablo Vista on State 20.

Y) NEWHALEM CREEK NCNP CAMP
129 campsites, trailers to 22', no hookups, flush toilets, wheelchair access, trailer waste disposal, on Skagit River, fishing, hiking, in North Cascades National Park, $10/night.

Southwest of Newhalem about 1 mile.

Z) CLARK'S SKAGIT RIVER RV PARK
64 units, 50 w/full hookups, 6 w/out hookups, plus 8 tent sites, reservation information - (206)873-2250, showers, laundry, restaurant, river, fishing, hiking, wildlife, $10 to $15/night.

Located 6 miles east of Rockport on State 20.

AA) HOWARD MILLER STEELHEAD PARK
70 campsites, 60 w/water & electricity, plus 10 tent sites, information - (206)853-8808, wheelchair access, picnic shelter, showers, playground, trailer waste disposal, river, swimming, fishing, boat launch, hiking, pets okay, $10 to $14/night.

At Rockport take Alfred Street to park.

BB) ROCKPORT STATE PARK
59 units, 50 w/full hookups, picnic shelter, wheelchair access includes old growth trail, trailer waste disposal, fishing, pets okay, $10 to $15/night.

Barely northwest of Rockport on State 20.

CC) CREEKSIDE CAMPING
27 campsites, 11 w/full hookups, 13 w/water & electricity, plus 3 w/no hookups, pets okay, reservations - (206)826-3566, showers, laundry, groceries, playground, trailer waste disposal, stream, fishing, $15/night.

Take State 20 7 miles west of Concrete, and follow Baker Lake Road north .2 mile to campground.

DD) BURLINGTON/CASCADE KOA
120 campsites, 52 w/full hookups, 10 w/water & electricity, 18 w/electricity, plus 40 tent units, reservations - (206)724-5511, wheelchair access, showers, laundry, cable tv, propane, indoor pool, sauna, hot tubs, rec room, playfield, playground, trailer waste disposal, stream, fishing, $17 to $23/night.

At Burlington, take Cook Road to Old Highway 99 and head north 3.5 miles to campground.

EE) RIVERBEND PARK
105 campsites, 75 w/full hookups, plus 30 tent units, information - (206)428-4044, wheelchair access, showers, laundry, rec room, trailer waste disposal, river, fishing, $12 to $17/night.

Go south of Burlington on I-5 to exit #227, and take College Way west .01 mile to Freeway Drive. Campground is .5 mile north.

FF) BAYVIEW STATE PARK
78 units, 9 w/full hookups, community kitchen, on Padilla Bay, play area, $10 to $16/night.

Take State 20 west of Burlington 6 miles; campground is 1.3 miles north of highway.

GG) DECEPTION PASS STATE PARK
246 units, some trailers - no hookups, community kitchen, wheelchair access, trailer waste disposal, boat launch, fishing, scuba diving area, swimming, pets okay, $10 to $11/night.

Deception State Park is located at the northern end of Whidbey Island, on State 20.

HH) FORT EBEY STATE PARK
50 units, some trailers - no hookups, wheelchair accessible, beach access, fishing, $10 to $11/night.

Fort Ebey State Park is located on the west side of Whidbey Island, about 6 miles northwest of Coupeville.

II) FORT CASEY STATE PARK
35 units, some trailers - no hookups, wheelchair access, boat launch, fishing, scuba diving, beach access, $10 to $11/night.

Take State 20 south of Coupeville 3.5 miles, and drive west 4.5 miles to campground.

JJ) SOUTH WHIDBEY STATE PARK
56 sites, some trailers - no hookups, wheelchair access, trailer waste disposal, scuba diving area, fishing, $10/night.

Leave Coupeville on State 20, and follow State 525 for about 6 miles. You'll see a road there leading to the campground.

KK) SILVER SHORES RV PARK
107 campsites, 87 w/full hookups, 8 w/water & electricity, plus 12 tent sites, reservations - (206)337-8741, showers, laundry, rec room, tennis, trailer waste disposal, small pets only, on Silver Lake, swimming, fishing, $10 to $20/night.

In Everett, at 11621 West Silver Lake Road.

PLEASE NOTE: There are over 100 campgrounds along the Cascade Loop, and dozens more just off the main route. The campgrounds listed here are among the largest. If you are looking for a smaller, or more primitive campground, check the listings in **Free Campgrounds of Washington & Oregon**, and **A Camper's Guide to Oregon & Washington**.

Camping
Vacation
#3

High Mountain Trekking
in the Steens

FROM THE AUTHOR'S JOURNAL . . .

No matter how many times I visit the Steens Mountain area I am never disappointed, for the beauty never pales, even when measured against a memory.

This year, with the wildflowers in full bloom, I find myself looking out over mountain meadows with enough color to put a Van Gogh to shame. It's hard to imagine this land once covered with glaciers, and the force with which they traveled, but the landscape they left behind gives silent testimony to their size and power.

Although we are here at a time when vacationers fill the roads elsewhere, this high mountain road is relatively empty. We pass only a few other kindred souls. Even though Jenica has spent nearly every one of her 16 summers camping the Pacific Northwest with me, this is the trip that leads her to say "Mom, when I have my own family we're going to spend all of our summers traveling just like this."

Our tour of the Malheur Wildlife Refuge was great. I let Jenica practice driving while I looked for wildlife. We must have stopped a hundred times to photograph deer resting along the creek, watch a flock of waterfowl, or to catch a better look at some small critter that had just run across the road. I've probably visited every wildlife refuge in the two-state area, but I always see more wildlife at Malheur than anywhere else.

Notes from a family vacation

HIGH MOUNTAIN TREKKING
IN THE STEENS

Oregon's highest road is found within the Steens Mountains, 60 miles south of Burns.

Known as the Steens Mountain Loop, this is not a super-highway, but a road taken merely for its scenic value. Along its route, you will encounter stunning views of glacially carved gorges and become acquainted with the austere beauty of the high desert country.

Commonly referred to as "The Steens", these mountains were created 15 million years ago when a 30-mile-long fault block was shoved upward through the cooling volcanic mass.

This basalt mountain was drastically altered during the Ice Age, when mammoth glaciers gouged their way through its valleys. These glaciers left behind magnificent U-shaped gorges and a spectacular countryside.

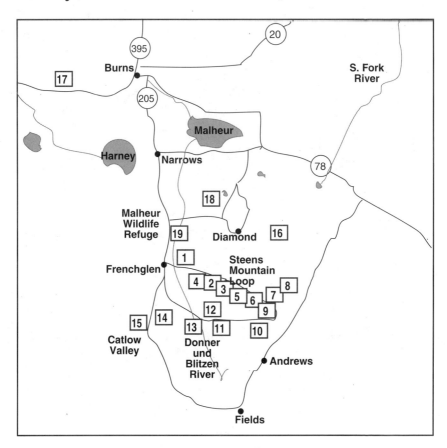

Steens Area Recreational Attractions

Located within the Great Basin, the mountain's rugged eastern face towers high above the flat Alvord Desert. The western side makes a more gradual descent.

The Bureau of Land Management operates three public campgrounds on Steens Mountain. All have potable water and restroom facilities, but offer little else in the way of creature comforts. A couple of privately operated campgrounds near the base of the mountain provide space for those who want a more civilized camping experience.

Steens Mountain includes 775,600 acres, and has an elevation of 9,773 feet. About 70% of its land is managed by the BLM; 100,000 of those acres are classified recreational.

Traveling the Steens Mountain Loop
The **Steens Mountain Loop [1]** is a 66 mile unpaved roadway. Visitors should allow at least 4 hours to make the entire drive, but the scenery is so inviting that you really should plan on an entire day. The road is not recommended for low clearance vehicles, RVs or trailers.

The upper road is closed from late October to mid-June; lower elevation sections are generally open from late spring until winter snow falls. Parts of this loop are steep and narrow, but most family cars have no problem navigating the lower portion. It has plenty of safe turn-arounds, should you decide the road has become too steep or rough for your vehicle.

Even if you only drive the short distance to Kiger Gorge Viewpoint, it's a worthwhile trip. The mountain scenery is spectacular. At 5,500 feet the landscape changes from a sagebrush dotted terrain to a rocky one filled with steep rimmed canyons.

The Aspen Belt, from 6,500 to 8,000 feet, is where you'll find groves of quaking aspen, mountain mahogany and isolated small meadows. The Alpine Bunchgrass Belt begins at 8,000 feet, and is the most sensational with its pristine high country, open meadows and glaciated valleys.

In the mountains, upper elevation temperatures can drop into the low 20s at night; during the daytime they normally reach the 70s.

The North Loop Route
The Steens Mountain Loop begins at Frenchglen, near the Page Springs Campground. From there you travel across the Blitzen River and take the North Loop Road up the mountain. This route will take you past Lily, Fish, Page and Honeymoon Lakes, by Whorehouse Meadows, and along the head of Kiger Gorge.

A few mountain lakes are all that remain of the ancient glaciers and numerous ice fields that once covered this land. Over the centuries, most of the

glacially created lakes have disappeared, filled in by plants and sediment. A lot of the meadows you see along the way were once lakes. **Lily Lake [2]**, near the beginning of the loop drive, is a living example of how those lakes were consumed.

Fish Lake [3], a few miles beyond Lily, is popular with campers who like to fish. This glacial pocket is at an elevation of 7,000 feet, and stocked with rainbow and eastern brook cutthroat trout. You'll find it just off the road. Wildhorse Lake, several miles further, is the only other lake within The Steens that is large enough to support fish. Several mountain streams offer year round trout fishing.

Corral Creek [4], **Honeymoon Lake [5]** and **Whorehouse Meadows [6]** date back to the Roaring

Twenties. This was a time when local cowboys, and Basque and Irish sheepherders, brought their livestock up the mountain to summer on its cooler pastures. The upper elevation aspen groves were where the men gathered for music and revelry. At that time, more than 100,000 animals were said to have grazed on the mountain during the summers; today only 10,000 cattle are allowed.

At the **Kiger Gorge Overlook [7]** you'll enjoy an expansive view that includes the Alvord Basin. If you are experiencing any worry about driving the mountain loop, this is a good place to turn around. If not, you will still have plenty of opportunities up ahead.

The **"Big Nick" [8]**, between Kiger Gorge and House Creek, is the only place where the main rim was completely eroded away. At other spots the rim was reduced to just a few hundred feet. This area has a number of small lakes where glaciers once sat.

Continuing along the loop, the road will become rougher but your reward will be spectacular views of the **Little Blitzen River [9]**, traveling along the Rooster Comb, and a chance to explore Little Blitzen and Big Indian Canyons.

There is a primitive road just past Little Blitzen Gorge that you can hike to reach **Wildhorse Lake [10]**. The lake is stocked with Lahontan cutthroat trout. Wildhorse sits in a hanging valley, an oasis created by a second series of glaciers. Those glaciers formed at the top of the gorge and pushed fresh earth down the basalt landscape. When they melted, they left behind this beautiful isolated dirt-filled valley.

The South Loop Route

Big Indian [11] and **Little Blitzen Gorges [12]** were once filled with rivers of ice. The loop road winds along the narrow ridge that separates the heads of these canyons from the mountain's sheer eastern face. From there, the South Loop Road follows the hogback that separates the two rivers, takes you down the face of another fault, and travels below the Rooster Comb.

The mountain's **Donner und Blitzen River [13]** has been designated wild and scenic. Its protected waters include Fish Creek, and the creeks running down Little Blitzen and Big Indian Gorge.

Continuing on, you will encounter several more scenic viewpoints before making your way down the mountain to **Catlow Valley [14]** and Highway 205. You rejoin the highway 10 miles south of Frenchglen.

The Steens are home to a variety of wildlife, so be sure to bring your binoculars. Bighorn sheep frequent the east rim; they are spectacular with their massive, curled horns. Mule deer and Rocky Mountain elk are also easy to spot; particularly at dawn and dusk.

Pronghorn antelope, America's fastest mammal, are often seen grazing along the mountain. Although they prefer the sagebrush of the lower elevation, it is also not uncommon to see them near the top.

Wild horses frequent the plateau area between **Catlow Rim [15]** and the Blitzen River. This herd currently includes about 300 horses, and is monitored by the BLM to preserve their free-roaming spirit. Coyotes, bobcats, mountain lions, black-tailed jackrabbits and beaver also live on the mountain.

Golden eagles, hawks, and falcons soar overhead in search of food, riding the rim's wind currents. Sage grouse, mourning dove, quail, chukar partridge, owls and songbirds are all plentiful. You'll find the best birdwatching in the alpine uplands.

In the early summer the mountain landscape is bright with wildflowers. They begin to bloom in April at lower elevations, and by the time those start to fade, flowers begin appearing at higher elevations. Along the high road wildflowers blossom into mid-summer. The colors of fall too are grand here, especially in the Aspen Belt.

Low Elevation Attractions
You can also drive clear around the mountain's base for a different perspective of The Steens. To do this, follow Highway 205 to Frenchglen, take the county road through Catlow Valley, Fields and Andrews, and then follow Highway 78 back to 205.

There's a lot more to a Steens Mountain vacation than just seeing the mountain. You can watch the wild mustang herd that grazes southeast of Diamond, or take a tour of the BLM wild horse corrals west of Burns. Visit Diamond Craters for a look at North America's largest variety of basaltic volcanic features, or enjoy lunch at the historic Frenchglen Hotel before an afternoon in the Malheur National Wildlife Refuge.

To reach the **Kiger Mustang Viewing Area [16]**, take Highway 205 north of Frenchglen to the turnoff for Diamond. Follow this road past the town, and on up the grade. At the top, turn right where the sign points to an unimproved road and drive 11 miles to where the wild mustangs graze.

When these herds get too large for the range, some are captured and placed for adoption through the BLM Adopt-A-Horse Program. These animals are tamed at the BLM **wild horse corrals [17]** on the north side of Highway 20, west of Burns. Stop in at the BLM office for permission to visit the corrals.

Diamond Craters [18] has lots of unusual lava formations. To find them, take the Diamond turnoff and follow the signs. There are no tourist facilities along this paved road, so check the gas gauge before you leave. The BLM offers a self-guided tour brochure to help you explore the domes, craters and other features of Diamond Craters.

If you like wildlife, you'll definitely want to spend some time at the **Malheur National Wildlife Refuge [19]**. Mule deer are easy to spot along the Donner und Blitzen Canal. Coyote, raccoon, weasel, mink, badger, porcupine, muskrat and jackrabbits are also common.

Herons, waterfowl, vultures, hawks, falcon, eagles, owls and songbirds are regular visitors. You might also see white pelican, cormorant, snowy egrets, whistling and trumpeter swans, and sandhill cranes.

This wetland area has been a major nesting place, and migratory stopover, since prehistoric times. The little museum at the refuge headquarters is a favorite with kids. It provides an opportunity to examine stuffed birds, nests and eggs up close.

A vacation in the Steens Mountains is a good way to get in touch with the state's beginnings. From prehistoric volcanoes and glaciers to 19th century sheep and cattle ranching, it all happened here.

For Additional Information
A phone call to the Burns area Bureau of Land Management (BLM) office will get you lots of information on this area. Be sure to ask for the Diamond Craters self-guided tour brochure as well as information on the Steens Mountain Loop.

BLM – Burns Office .... (503) 573-5241

Malheur Wildlife Refuge .... (503) 573-6582

Steens Area Campgrounds

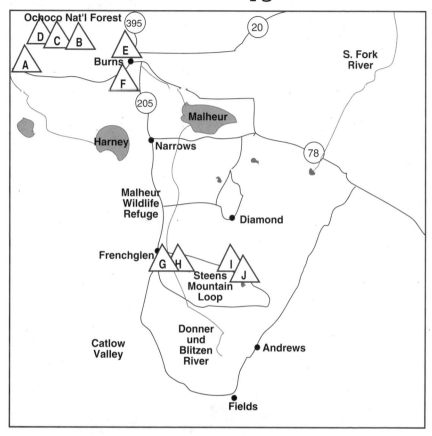

A) CHICKAHOMINY BLM RECREATION SITE
Open camp area, vault toilets, drinking water, picnic facilities, lake fishing, boating, boat ramp, no fee.

West of Burns 34 miles on US 20.

B) FALLS FS CAMP
5 units, trailers to 22', well water, pit toilets, stream fishing, in Ochoco NF, pets okay, $4/night.

Northwest of Burns, via FSR 47 for 15 miles, then FSR 41 an additional 18 miles.

C) EMIGRANT FS CAMP
6 units, trailers to 22', well water - not always drinkable, pit toilets, stream fishing, in Ochoco NF, $0 to $4/night.

Northwest of Burns, via FSR 47 for 15 miles, then FSR 41 an additional 20.0 miles.

D) DELINTMENT LAKE FS CAMP
24 units, trailers to 22', picnic area, well water, pit toilets – handicap accessible, handicap accessible fishing dock, boat launch, boating, fishing, in Ochoco NF, pets okay, $6/night.

Northwest of Burns, via FSR 47 for 15 miles, then FSR 41 an additional 25 miles to FSR 4365. Take this west 3 miles to FSR 41, and go an additional 5 miles west to campground.

E) VILLAGE TRAILER PARK
41 campsites w/full hookups, reservation information - (503)573-7640, showers, laundry, river, $11 to $17/night.

Located in Burns, just off US 395/20, at 1273 Seneca Drive.

F) SANDS TRAILER PARK
16 campsites, 10 w/full hookups, plus 6 tent units, reservation information - (503)573-7010, showers, $8 to $10/night.

This campground is 1 mile south of Burns on US 395/20.

G) STEENS MOUNTAIN RESORT CAMP & CAMPER CORRAL
75 campsites, 55 w/full hookups, 202 w/water & electricity, plus large tent area, reservation information - (503)493-2415, fire pits, showers, laundry, trailer waste disposal, river, swimming, fishing, hiking, elev. 4100', $10 to $14/night.

Located 3 miles southeast of Frenchglen, on Fishlake Road.

H) PAGE SPRINGS BLM CAMP
30 units, trailers to 24', water, hiking, borders on Malheur Wildlife Refuge, fishing, elev. 4339', $3.00/night.

Located 4 miles southeast of Frenchglen, on the Blitzen River.

I) FISH LAKE BLM CAMP
20 units, trailers to 24', lake, well water, hiking trails, boat dock, boating, swimming, trout fishing, elev. 7500', $4/vehicle.

Located 17 miles east of Frenchglen, on the northern portion of the Steens Mountain Loop.

J) JACKMAN BLM PARK
5 units, water, hiking, bird watching, elev. 8100', $4,00/vehicle.

Located 20 miles east of Frenchglen on the northern portion of the Steens Mountain Loop.

If the BLM campgrounds are full, you can generally camp elsewhere, as long as you don't drive off the road, stay out of areas that are posted closed, and practice "no trace" camping so that no one will be able to tell you were there after you leave.

Camping
Vacation
#4

Kites, Sunken Ships, Old Forts, and a Drive on the World's Longest Beach

FROM THE AUTHOR'S JOURNAL . . .

*As the music began playing over the loud speakers,
eight kites moved upward, flipped over, and turned
right with the beat. Each duplicated the movements of
its neighbor with the precision of a military marching
unit. Several minutes later, the music ended and, as it
did, all eight kites came to rest on the beach in a
perfectly straight line.*

*We gazed upward for the next two days, watching one
beautifully choreographed performance after another as
kite enthusiasts from near and far competed in
Washington's annual international kite festival. The
bright colors, interesting shapes, and seemingly
effortless teamwork were memorable.*

*I had visited the Long Beach Peninsula countless times
in the past, but always before, it had been to enjoy the
seemingly endless ocean beaches. We spent very little
time walking the beach on this trip. I knew that the
beaches would be there next week, but this unusual
festival would not happen again for another year.*

*Of course we did manage to squeeze in a visit to
Marsh's Museum. This is one Long Beach attraction my
family has to visit every time we're in town. Its eclectic
collection of whimsy, antiques and souvenirs never gets
boring. Pushing coins into the old-fashioned music
machines, we are instantly transported to a time when
things were built to last, as we watch and listen to the
world's first jukeboxes.*

Notes from a Washington coast weekend

KITES, SUNKEN SHIPS, OLD FORTS, AND A DRIVE ON THE WORLD'S LONGEST BEACH

71

Kite-flying is a popular pastime with Long Beach Peninsula visitors, making it a great place for a family vacation. Almost any time of year, the skies are filled with bright colors and interesting shapes.

The peninsula's steady breezes have made it the location of a special event for kite enthusiasts since 1981. Held in mid August, the **Washington State International Kite Festival [1]** draws competitors from all over the world for seven days of activities.

Brightly colored kite trains, lighted stunt kites, and an array of one-of-a-kind, box and handcrafted kites crowd the skies. Workshops for beginning and advanced flyers are offered, along with daily demonstrations. On the final day, there's a Festival of Kites, an attempt to break the Western Hemisphere record for the most kites in the sky at one time.

The Long Beach Peninsula is also where you'll find the **world's longest beach [2]**. Its 28-mile length gives visitors unlimited ocean access. Camping is not allowed on the beach, but campers will find plenty of places to stay along the peninsula.

Washington's ocean beaches are considered highways, which means you can drive most of the peninsula's shoreline. Follow the same rules you would on any other state highway. Be sure to keep your car below the high tide line, on the wet sand; driving on higher ground will get your vehicle stuck in the soft sand.

The waters off the Long Beach Peninsula are littered with sunken ships; hundreds have disappeared here during the past 270 years. In fact, this area is known as 'the graveyard of the Pacific'. Schooners, sloops, steamers, trollers, brigs, gunboats and numerous other ships have been lost to its treacherous currents.

Exploring the Peninsula's Historic Beginnings
When Captain Gray landed on the north shore of the Columbia River in 1792, his visit launched the American claim to the northwest coast. Lewis and Clark arrived in November of 1805, and reported this area as being inhabited by Chief Comcomally and his tribe. They lived in communal long houses along the Columbia River and the peninsula's Willapa Bay.

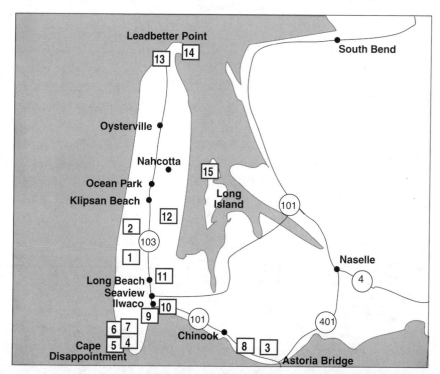

Long Beach Peninsula Attractions

You can visit the **Lewis and Clark Expedition camp-site [3]**. A marker near St. Mary's Church, along the Columbia River just west of the Astoria bridge, identifies this historic spot. A second monument in Long Beach, at Highway 103 and Third Street, marks the most northwestern point visited by the expedition.

The **Lewis and Clark Interpretive Center [4]** at Fort Canby State Park chronicles the group's 8,000-mile journey. It paints a vivid picture of the people involved, and the hardships they suffered. There is no charge to tour the center. It takes less than an hour and is handicap-accessible. You'll find it open daily throughout the summer, and on weekends the rest of the year, from 9:00 a.m. to 5:00 p.m.

The center also has information on the construction of the cape's two lighthouses and Fort Canby. The **Cape Disappointment [5]** and **North Head Lighthouses [6]** are still standing, and were built in 1856 and 1899.

Fort Canby [7] was the state's first coastal defense installation, and was in active use from 1875 to 1957. Kids of all ages enjoy exploring the fort's old bunkers,

and the interpretive center sits on the site of two of the original defense batteries. From here, your view of Cape Disappointment is the same one those early explorers saw when they first reached the Pacific Ocean.

Fort Canby State Park's 2,000 acres provide the public with hiking trails, picnic facilities, campsites, ocean beaches, great birdwatching areas, good fishing, and whale watching. Salmon, rock cod, lingcod, flounder, perch and sea bass are caught in the surrounding waters.

The waters off Cape Disappointment are dangerous, and swimming there is unsafe. Fort Canby's Waikiki Beach is probably the safest spot, but be careful and stay close to shore. During the winter, storms bring huge green waves crashing over the rocks of Cape Disappointment, shooting water a hundred feet into the air.

Fort Columbia [8] was built around 1897 and remains in near-original condition. It now serves as a state park, providing visitors with the opportunity to see what military life was like in the U.S. Army's coastal artillery corps around the turn of the century.

The park includes a number of military bunkers, batteries and lookouts, plus 14 wooden buildings, a guardhouse, barracks, hospital, supply building, and other structures. The displays and museum exhibits are both fun and educational.

Fort Columbia State Park is two miles west of the Astoria Bridge, on Highway 101. You can explore the grounds daily during the summer; they are closed on Mondays and Tuesdays the balance of the year.

Things To Do, Places To Go

If you like boats, stop by the **Ilwaco boat basin [9]**. Tuna boats, trawlers, shrimpers, salmon trollers, crabbers, charter and privately owned boats line its docks. This is an exciting place to be when the boats come in with the day's catch. Dockside canneries sell fresh seafood, and many welcome visitors.

If you'd like to learn more about local history, visit the **Ilwaco Heritage Museum [10]**, on Lake Street. You'll find it open from 9:00 a.m. to 4:00 p.m. Monday through Saturday, and noon to 4:00 p.m. on Sunday.

The museum's most popular exhibit is a 50-foot-long miniature railroad. An exact replica of the 1920 Ilwaco Railroad and Navigation Company's local line, its landscape includes exact copies of local buildings and thousands of tiny trees. Other museum exhibits highlight local Indians, pioneer life, the fur trade, and coastal explorers.

The town of Long Beach is always popular with families. It has an amusement center, go-karts, bumper cars, kiddie rides, lots of interesting shops, and **Marsh's Free Museum [11]**.

Marsh's is best described as a combination side show, antique game room, second-hand store, gift shop. You'll find freak-show oddities that include two-headed animals, Jake the alligator man, shrunken heads, and an array of bizarre man-made creatures.

You can operate antique juke boxes, peep shows and old-time game machines. Even small children, and people who think museums are boring, will spend hours at Marsh's.

A series of brightly painted murals decorate the buildings of Ilwaco, Long Beach, Chinook and Nahcotta. They depict turn-of-the-century street scenes, farming, fishing, cranberry harvests, and other historic events. These huge outdoor canvasses bring color and artistry to the towns.

Driving towards the peninsula's north end, you'll find **Loomis Lake State Park [12]** just past Cranberry Road. Loomis Lake is the largest of the numerous lakes that occupy the peninsula's center. Trumpeter Swans nest here in the winter; summer brings trout anglers, canoeists, and picnickers.

Leadbetter Point State Park [13], on the peninsula's northern tip, is popular with birdwatchers. Over 100 species of birds visit this refuge, including black brandt and snowy plover. Other park activities include surf fishing, digging for clams, beachcombing, and hiking along dune and forest trails. The open dune area at the very tip is part of the **Willapa National Wildlife Refuge [14]**.

Long Island [15], in Willapa Bay, is also part of the wildlife refuge. This island is probably best known as the site of the United States' last stand of old-growth red cedar. You'll need your own boat to reach the island. Cross the channel at Nahcotta and you'll find a 2.5-mile trail leading to the 274-acre grove of ancient trees. These trees range in diameter from five to eleven feet and have an average height of 160 feet.

But there's more to Long Island than just the ancient trees. This is the Pacific Coast's largest estuarine island. Natural inhabitants include deer, bear, elk, beaver, otter, and a variety of birds. Canoeing, kayaking, hiking, birdwatching and limited camping are available. Visitors need to carry their own water and pack out anything they pack in.

Camping on the island is only for those who respect nature, and is restricted to a handful of established campsites. High tide plays an important role in campground accessibility, so check with the Willapa Wildlife Refuge officials before assuming you'll find a place to pitch your tent.

For Additional Information
If you want to plan your camping trip to coincide with one of the peninsula's many festivals, check with the Long Beach Peninsula Visitors Bureau. The people there can provide you with information on a number of fun happenings. Most offer a variety of family activities, and focus on local products. Popular events include an annual sand-sculpture contest, garlic festival, and of course, the Washington State International Kite Festival.

Long Beach Peninsula
    Visitors Bureau .... (800) 451-2542

Lewis & Clark Interpretive Center .... (206) 753-5755

Fort Canby State Park .... (206) 753-5755

Fort Columbia State Park .... (206) 777-8221
    also .... (206) 777-8358

Willapa National Wildlife Refuge .... (206) 484-3482

Long Beach Peninsula Campgrounds

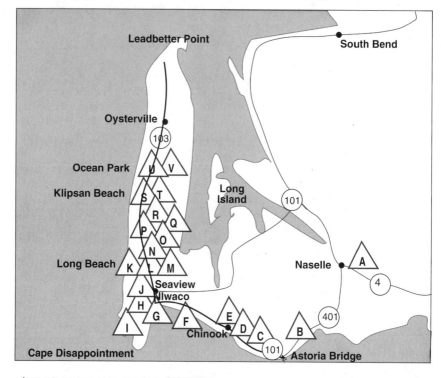

A) NASALLE TRAILER COURT
24 trailer sites w/full hookups, no tents, reservation information - (206)484-3351, showers, laundry, $15/night.

Northeast of Ilwaco. US 101 southeast 10 miles, State 401 north 12 miles, State 4 southeast 1.5 miles.

B) CHRIS'S RV PARK & CAMPGROUND
100 units, 64 w/water & electricity, 16 w/out hookups, plus 20 tent sites, reservation information - (206)777-8475, showers, laundry, rec room w/tv, trailer waste disposal, picnic facilities, river, fishing, $10 to $14/night.

Take State 401 3 miles north of its junction with US 101.

C) MAUCH'S SUNDOWN RV PARK
59 campsites, 49 w/full hookups, plus 10 w/water & electricity, reservation information - (206)777-8713, showers, laundry, trailer waste disposal, on river, fishing, $10 to $12/night.

Located just west of the Astoria Bridge, on US 101.

D) RIVER'S END CAMPGROUND
100 campsites, 20 w/full hookups, 40 w/water & electricity, plus 40 tent sites, reservation information - (206)777-8317, showers, laundry, rec room, playground, trailer waste disposal, river, fishing, $16 to $20/night.

Located just south of Chinook, on US 101.

E) CHINOOK COUNTY PARK
100 campsites (some w/hookups, plus hike-in & tent sites), reservation information - (206)777-8442, showers, playground, river, $5 to $14/night.

Located in Chinook, at east end of town.

F) ILWACO KOA
200 campsites, 36 w/full hookups, 90 w/electricity only, plus 74 tent units, reservations - (206)642-3292, showers, laundry, groceries, trailer waste disposal, playground, rec room, ocean access, near Columbia River, fishing, $16 to $21/night.

Located on US 101, between Ilwaco and Chinook.

G) THE BEACON RV PARK
60 campsites, 40 w/full hookups, plus 20 w/electricity only, reservation information - (206)642-2138, no tents, showers, cable tv, river, fishing, pets okay, $13 to $15/night.

In Ilwaco, at east end of docks.

H) COVE RV PARK
40 units w/full hookups (6 are pull-thrus), no tent sites, pets welcome, reservation information - (206)642-3689, showers, laundry, trailer waste disposal, by Baker Bay, $15/night.

In Ilwaco, at west end of port area.

I) FORT CANBY STATE PARK
254 units, 60 w/full hookups, wheelchair access, groceries, trailer waste disposal, boat launch, fishing, interpretive center, ocean access, trails, $10 to $15/night.

Located 2.5 miles southwest of Ilwaco.

J) SOU'WESTER LODGE & TRAILER PARK
60 campsites w/full hookups, reservation information - (206)642-2542, showers, laundry, ocean access, fishing, $$$.

Leave US 101 just south of Seaview, on Seaview Beach Road, and head west 1 block to park.

K) SAND CASTLE RV PARK
38 campsites, 29 w/full hookups, no tents, reservations - (206)642-2174, showers, laundry, ocean access, $15 to $16/night.

In Long Beach, right on State 103.

L) ANTHONY'S HOME COURT
25 campsites w/full hookups, reservation information - (206)642-2802, showers, laundry, fish cleaning area, $12 to $15/night.

In Long Beach, at 1310 Pacific Highway North.

M) DRIFTWOOD RV TRAV-L-PARK
50 campsites w/full hookups, plus 4 tent units, reservations - (206)642-2711, showers, cable tv, laundry, ocean access, fishing, $15/night.

In Long Beach, right on State 103.

N) SAND-LO MOTEL & TRAILER PARK
15 campsites w/full hookups, plus 4 tent sites - no fire pits, reservations - (206)642-2600, showers, laundry, restaurant, groceries, fish cleaning area, $14/night.

North of Long Beach 1 mile, right on State 103.

O) PACIFIC PARK TRAILER PARK
50 trailer sites, 44 w/full hookups, plus 6 w/water & electricity, no tent sites, reservation information - (206)642-3253, showers, laundry, ocean access, $15/night.

North of Long Beach 2 miles on State 103.

P) CRANBERRY TRAILER PARK
24 trailer sites w/full hookups, no tents, adults only, reservations - (206)642-2027, showers, rec room, cable tv, $10/night.

Take State 103 north of Long Beach 3 miles to Cranberry Road and head east .3 mile.

Q) ANDERSEN'S TRAILER COURT
71 units, 56 w/full hookups, plus 15 tent sites, reservations - (800) 645-6795, showers, cable tv, laundry, trailer waste disposal, ocean access, fishing, playground, $11 to $14/night.

North of Long Beach 3.5 miles on State 103.

R) PEGG'S OCEANSIDE RV PARK
30 campsites w/full hookups, no tents, reservation information - (206)642-2451, showers, ocean access, rec room, cable tv, laundry, $12 to $14/night.

North of Long Beach 4.5 miles on State 103.

S) EVERGREEN COURT
36 campsites, 30 w/full hookups, 6 tent units, plus large dry camp area, reservation information - (206)665-5100, showers, playground, trailer waste disposal, $8 to $10/night.

North of Long Beach 7.9 miles on State 103, located just north of 22nd Street.

T) WESTGATE RV PARK & MOTEL
36 sites w/full hookups, no tents, reservation information - (206)665-4211, showers, rec room, ocean access, fishing, fish cleaning room, $13 to $14/night.

At Klipsan Beach.

U) OCEAN PARK RESORT
100 campsites, 94 w/full hookups, plus 6 w/water & electricity, reservation (800)835-4634, showers, cable tv, laundry, rec room, swimming pool, hot tub, playground, $14.50/night.

In Ocean Park, .1 mile east of the highway, on 259th Street.

V) OCEAN AIRE TRAILER PARK
46 trailer sites w/full hookups, no tents, trailers to 35', reservation information - (206)665-4027, showers, laundry, $13/night.

In Ocean Park, about .1 mile east of the highway, on 260th Street.

Camping
Vacation
#5

Picturesque Encounters
at the Oregon Coast

FROM THE AUTHOR'S JOURNAL . . .

Like most Oregonians, I have taken plenty of day trips, weekend excursions and summer vacations along the beautiful Oregon coast. So many that it is often easier to sort them out by reflecting on the company or activities rather than where they actually took place.

I've enjoyed the fun-filled atmosphere of the northern coast, taken part in the fellowship of coastal artistic communities, been awed by the spectacular beauty of the southern coastline, and spent time in every park along its shores.

But when asked what I like best about the Oregon coast, it can only be one thing. It's not the solitude of an early morning walk along a deserted beach, the cool glow of the sunset as it drops into the Pacific Ocean, or the feeling of community that comes with time spent in one of its many charming towns. Though these are all special, what I like best about the Oregon coast, is the romance.

For me, Lincoln City will always be the Oregon coast's most romantic town. It's a town that caters to lovers. John and I were married on one of Lincoln City's beautiful beaches, at high tide, as the sun gently melted into the ocean. No matter how hard you try, it's hard to top that for romance!

Reflections on a lifetime of coastal vacations

PICTURESQUE ENCOUNTERS AT THE OREGON COAST

The Oregon coast belongs to everyone. Unlike all of the other coastal states, where most of humanity is restricted to a few overcrowded beaches and wealthy landowners build fences to keep others from invading

Oregon Coast Attractions

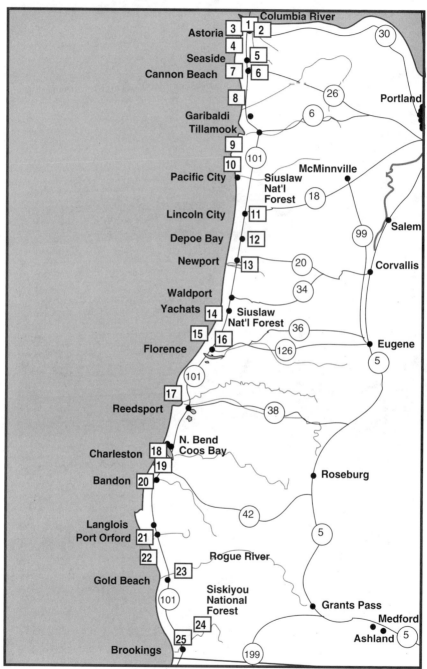

"their" ocean, nearly all of Oregon's beaches are public. This gives the state 360 miles of spectacular coastal parks.

Campers will find thousands of individual campsites to choose from along the coast. Head inland a bit and you'll discover even more. In total, this region has more than 200 public campgrounds, which will accommodate up to 11,000 families at one time.

The Oregon coastline varies. Some areas have mountains running right down to the sea, others flat sandy beaches. But best of all, no matter where you go, you'll find plenty of small, secluded beaches. Most are accessible to any visitors willing to hike a bit.

Day-use state and local parks make it easy for the public to enjoy the ocean. They showcase sparkling white sand dunes, agate-strewn beaches, surf-carved caves, forested capes, offshore monoliths, old growth forests, giant rhododendrons, and historic sites.

The North Coast
The northern Oregon coast, with its broad sandy beaches, is where America's west began. Astoria, on the Columbia River, was the first permanent U.S. settlement this side of the Rocky Mountains.

Some of Astoria's early buildings still stand, including **Flavel House [1]**. This elegant 1883 Victorian-style home was built by a local sea captain. For a small fee you can tour the house between 11:00 a.m. and 4:00 p.m. Flavel House is at 8th and Duane Streets.

Astoria's **Columbia River Maritime Museum [2]** showcases 200 years of nautical history. You'll find lots of ship models, naval displays, and nautical artifacts inside. Outside, you can tour the west coast's last seagoing lighthouse, the lightship Columbia. Located on the waterfront, at 17th Street, and open daily from 9:30 a.m. to 5:00 p.m., the charge is minimal.

Fort Stevens [3] was an important military base from 1865 to 1947. Today it is a state park. You can tour the fort's old buildings and batteries year round, and in the summer they put on living history skits. The buildings are open daily from 10:00 a.m. to 6:00 p.m. in the summer; the rest of the year they are only open Wednesday thru Sunday and close at 4:00 p.m.

Photo Courtesy of The Friends of old Ft. Stevens

At **Fort Clatsop [4]**, 5 miles south of Astoria, you can tour a replica of Lewis and Clark's 1805 winter encampment. Open year round, from 8:00 a.m. to

5:00 p.m., the fort has been recreated, and exhibits explain the significance of this historic journey.

The north coast is full of interesting little resort towns, and a good family destination. The town of **Seaside [5]** sports a fun-filled promenade and is a favorite with summer visitors. **Cannon Beach [6]** is a charming artistic community popular with Northwest residents.

At **Ecola State Park [7]** you'll find a setting described by Lewis and Clark as *"the grandest and most pleasing prospect which my eyes have ever surveyed."* **Oswald West State Park [8]** protects a rain forest of massive spruce and cedar. Other outstanding state park attractions include **Cape Meares' Octopus Tree [9]**, and **Cape Kiwanda's tidepools [10]**.

The Central Coast
The central Oregon coast is also popular with vacationers. Defined as the land that lies between Cascade Head and Coos Bay, it too has lots of great family vacation spots.

The skies over **Lincoln City [11]** are always filled with kites. Beachcombers, waterskiers, windsurfers, and anglers are drawn to its seashore; shoppers like the factory outlet mall and quaint little shops.

Depoe Bay's **Devil's Churn [12]** is a wonderful natural attraction. At high tide this saltwater geyser spouts 60 feet into the air. Gray whales are also commonly spotted offshore here between December and May.

Newport [13] is where you'll find the wonderful new Oregon Coast Aquarium, Hatfield Marine Science Center, Ripley's Believe It or Not Museum, an undersea garden, and a wax museum. All are great family attractions, but if you don't have time to tour them all, you should at least allow time for the new aquarium.

The outdoor exhibits at the Oregon Coast Aquarium provide an opportunity to see seals, sea otters and puffin in near-natural surroundings. Indoors you'll find a beautifully lighted jellyfish tank, lots of hands-on exhibits, a great film on whales, and a whole lot more. The aquarium is open every day but Christmas, from 9:00 a.m. to 6:00 p.m., and the charge is $3.50 to $7.75, depending on your age.

Cape Perpetua [14], just south of Yachats, is a great place to learn what this area was like 40 million years ago. At the visitors' center you'll discover how the land evolved, see artifacts left behind by early Native Americans, retrace the region's discovery by non-natives, and inspect Indian shell midden. Interpretive trails and nature walks make this a fun place to visit.

The world famous **Sea Lion Caves [15]**, 10 miles south of the cape, is where you'll find a colony of Steller sea lions occupying America's largest sea cave. Visitors take an elevator down into the cave to where they can safely watch the one-ton mammals in their open-sea environment. Open year round, from 9:00 a.m. to just before dusk, the cost is $3.50 to $5.50.

Darlingtonia State Park [16], 5 miles north of Florence, has raised wooden walkways that allow you to stroll through a sea of unusual carnivorous plants.

The **Oregon Dunes National Recreation Area [17]** extends from Florence to Coos Bay. This 40-mile stretch is one of the largest coastal dune areas in the world. A number of parks line the area, making it a great vacation destination. You'll find miles of sparkling white sand dunes, great beaches for walking or sunbathing, protected wildlife areas, and lots of good hiking trails.

Dune buggy enthusiasts rank the Oregon Dunes among the West's most challenging. Even if you're not a participant, the buggies are fun to watch.

The South Coast
Oregon's south coast is where you'll find those forested mountains that begin right at the water's edge. Miles of unoccupied shoreland exist between the scattered towns, providing endless views of the ocean.

Shore Acres State Park [18], west of Coos Bay, is best known for its beautiful turn-of-the-century floral gardens. These gardens are all that's left of a beautiful old estate that once stood here. Attractions include a lovely Japanese garden, 100-foot lily pond, and a

spectacular collection of plants that were brought by sailing ships from all over the world. Outside the gardens, the sea pounds relentlessly against the sheer cliffs, creating a beautiful sculpted landscape.

Charleston is a popular charter fishing destination, and also where you'll find the **South Slough Estuary [19]**. Located four miles south of town, on Seven Devils Road, the estuary's trails and waterways can be enjoyed year round. During the summer, the interpretive center is open from 8:30 a.m. to 4:30 p.m. For a schedule of activities call (503) 888-5558.

Bandon [20] is a great spot for whale watching, and **Port Orford [21]** beaches are generally uncrowded. **Humbug Mountain State Park [22]**, 6 miles south of Port Orford, has a trail leading to the mountain's top that provides spectacular views of the coastline.

Gold Beach is situated at the mouth of the world-famous **Rogue River [23]**. A "wild and scenic" river, 84 miles of its pristine beauty are protected from further development. From the mouth of the Applegate River to Lobster Creek, you can tour the river only by boat or on foot. Tour boats operate on the lower part of the river, offering visitors a thrilling experience.

Loeb State Park [24], 10 miles east of Brookings, is situated along the Chetco River. This 320-acre setting is a wonderful place to spend the day, wandering thru large groves of myrtlewood and redwood trees. The redwood grove is the most northerly in the U.S.

Brookings is in Oregon's banana belt, so the temperature there is generally warmer than the rest of the coast. If you visit between April and July, stop at **Azalea State Park [25]** where you'll find 300-year-old azaleas in bloom. The colors are brilliant, making this a lovely spot for hiking or a quiet family picnic.

Between mid-May and the end of September, a $3.00 per day vehicle fee is charged at some of the most popular state parks. Seasonal permits are $20.00. If you camp in a state park, your receipt also serves as a day-use permit on the same day(s) you are registered for overnight camping.

The Oregon coast is a picture-perfect place for a family camping vacation. Whether you choose just one destination for your entire vacation, or spend your time wandering up and down the coastline, you're in for an unparalleled coastal experience.

For Additional Information

Visitor information centers are a great source for details on local attractions and activities. Call at least 3 weeks before your trip and you'll receive lots of brochure, maps, and other good information.

Visitor information centers –

Astoria	(503) 325-6311
Bandon	(503) 347-9616
Brookings Area	(800) 535-9469
Cannon Beach	(503) 436-2623
Coos Bay Area	(800) 824-8486
Depoe Bay	(503) 765-2889
Florence	(503) 997-3128
Gold Beach	(800) 525-2334
Lincoln City	(800) 452-2151
Newport	(800) 262-7844
Port Orford	(503) 332-8055
Seaside	(800) 444-6740

Tillamook .... (503) 842-7525
Waldport .... (503) 563-2133
Yachats .... (503) 547-3530

Oregon Coast Campgrounds

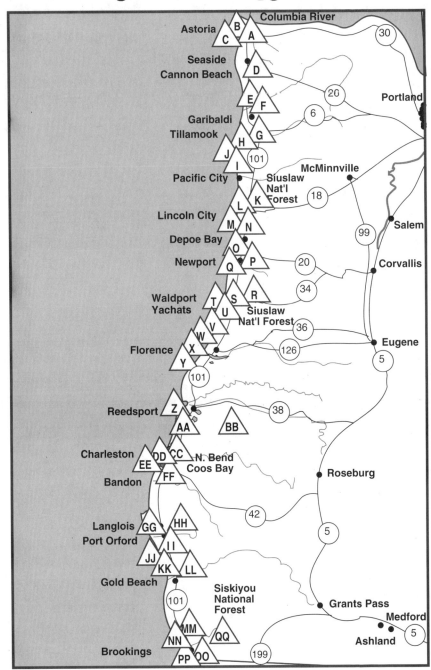

A) ASTORIA KOA
276 units, 142 w/full hookups, 87 w/water & electricity, plus 47 tent sites, reservations - (503)861-2606, showers, laundry, groceries, swimming pool, spa, playground, $18 to $25/night.

West of Astoria 10 miles, across from Fort Stevens State Park.

B) FORT STEVENS STATE PARK
605 campsites, 213 w/full hookups, 130 w/electricity , plus 262 tent units, mail-in reservations, maximum site 69', wheelchair access, picnic area, showers, trailer waste disposal, boat launch, fishing, ocean access, bicycle & hiking trails, $15 to $17/night.

West of Astoria 10 miles, near Warrenton.

C) KAMPERS WEST KAMPGROUND RV PARK
193 units, 137 w/full hookups, 50 w/water & electricity, plus 56 tent sites, reservation information - (503)861-1814, showers, laundry, trailer waste disposal, river, fishing, $13 to $17/night.

West of Astoria 10 miles – follow the Warrenton/Fort Stevens signs. Campground is located at 1140 NW Warrenton Drive.

D) RV RESORT AT CANNON BEACH
100 trailer sites w/full hookups, no tents, reservations - (503)436-2231, showers, laundry, cable tv, groceries, swimming pool, therapy pool, river, fishing, game room, playfield, playground, hiking, wheelchair access, $31/night.

At Cannon Beach – just off the Cannon Beach exit ramp; about .6 mile past milepost 29.

E) NEHALEM BAY STATE PARK
291 campsites w/electricity, maximum site 60', wheelchair access, picnic area, showers, trailer waste disposal, boat launch, fishing, ocean access, bicycle trail, horse trails, $10 to $16/night.

South of Cannon Beach 17 miles on US 101, campground is 3 miles south of Manzanita junction.

F) BAR VIEW JETTY COUNTY PARK
250 campsites, 40 w/full hookups, 20 w/electricity only, plus 190 tent units, reservation information - (503)322-3477, showers, trailer waste disposal, ocean access/swimming, fishing, playground, hiking, pets okay, $12 to $14/night.

North of Garibaldi 2 miles on US 101.

G) TILLAMOOK KOA
85 campsites, 21 w/full hookups, 53 w/water & electricity, plus 10 tent units, reservations - (503)842-4779, showers, laundry, groceries, playground, cable tv, trailer waste disposal, river, fishing, hiking, propane, $14 to $20/night.

South of Tillamook 6 miles on US 101.

H) CAPE LOOKOUT STATE PARK

250 campsites, 53 w/full hookups, plus 197 tent units, maximum site 60', mail reservations available, picnic area, wheelchair access, showers, trailer waste disposal, hiking trail, ocean beach, beachcombing, fishing, $15 to $17/night.

Southwest of Tillamook. Leave US 101 at Tillamook and head southwest 12 miles to campground.

I) CAPE KIWANDA RV PARK

159 campsites, 95 w/full hookups, 40 w/water & electricity, plus 24 tent sites, reservation information - (503)965-6230, showers, laundry, cable tv, groceries, trailer waste disposal, swimming, fishing, $12 to $17/night.

North of Pacific City. At city center take Brooten Road west .2 mile, then head north 1 mile to campground.

J) SAND BEACH NF CAMP

101 units, trailers to 32', flush toilets, trailer waste disposal, ORV area – dunes, boating, fishing, in Siuslaw NF, $8 to $12/night.

North of Pacific City. CR 536 west .2 mile, CR 535 north 8.4 miles, CR 503 west 1 mile, FSR S3001 southwest .5 mile.

K) LINCOLN CITY KOA

85 campsites, 23 w/full hookups, 29 w/water & electricity, plus 32 tent units, reservations - (503)994-2961, showers, laundry, groceries, game room, rec room w/kitchen, propane, trailer waste disposal, playground, pets okay, $15 to $17/night.

Northeast of Lincoln City. US 101 north 4 miles, East Devils Lake Road southeast 1 mile.

L) DEVIL'S LAKE STATE PARK

100 campsites, 32 w/full hookups, plus 68 tent units, mail reservations available, maximum site 62', wheelchair access, showers, boat launch, on East Devil's Lake, boating, fishing, swimming, $15 to $17/night.

In Lincoln City, just off US 101.

M) SEA & SAND RV PARK

95 campsites w/full hookups, no tents, trailers to 35', reservation information - (503)764-2313, wheelchair access, showers, laundry, trailer waste disposal, swimming, fishing, $17/night.

North of Depoe Bay 3.5 miles on US 101.

N) FOGARTY CREEK RV PARK

53 trailer sites w/full hookups, no tents, reservation information - (503)764-2228, showers, cable tv, laundry, trailer waste disposal, $14 to $18/night.

North of Depoe Bay 2 miles on US 101.

O) BEVERLY BEACH STATE PARK
279 campsites, 52 w/full hookups, 75 w/electricity, 152 tent units, plus hiker/biker camp, mail reservations available, maximum site 65', picnic area, wheelchair access, showers, trailer waste disposal, ocean access, hiking, $4 to $17/night.

North of Newport 7 miles on US 101.

P) HARBOR VILLAGE TRAILER PARK
140 trailer sites w/full hookups, no tents, information - (503)265-5088, showers, laundry, $14/night.

East of Newport .5 mile via US 20, SW Moore Drive south .5 mile, SE Bay Blvd. east 1 block.

Q) SOUTH BEACH STATE PARK
254 campsites w/electricity, plus hiker/biker camp, mail reservations available, maximum site 60', wheelchair access, showers, trailer waste disposal, ocean access, $4 to $16/night.

South of Newport 2 miles on US 101.

R) DRIFT CREEK LANDING
60 trailer sites, 52 w/full hookups, plus 8 w/water & electricity, no tents, information - (503)563-3610, showers, laundry, river, fishing, boat launch & rental, pets okay, $15 to $16/night.

East of Waldport 3.7 miles on State 34.

S) BEACHSIDE STATE PARK
80 campsites, 27 w/hookups for electricity, plus 54 tent units, mail reservations available, maximum site 30', picnic area, showers, ocean access, $15 to $16/night.

South of Waldport 4 miles on US 101.

T) TILLICUM BEACH NF CAMP
57 units, trailers to 32', piped water, flush toilets, ocean view campsites, fishing, in Siuslaw NF, pets okay, $10 to $15/night.

South of Waldport 4.7 miles on US 101.

U) CAPE PERPETUA NF CAMP
37 units, 1 group site, reservations required - (503)563-3211, trailers to 22', piped water, stream, flush toilets, trailer waste disposal, interpretive services, fishing, hiking, Pacific Ocean access, in Siuslaw NF, pets okay, $10 to $15/night.

South of Yachats 2.7 miles on US 101.

V) SEA PERCH RV PARK & CAMPGROUND
48 campsites, 21 w/full hookups, 27 w/water & electricity, plus 4 tent sites, reservations - (503)547-3505, showers, laundry, ocean access, swimming, fishing, pets okay, $15 to $22/night.

South of Yachats 6.5 miles on US 101.

W) SUTTON NF CAMPGROUND
90 campsites, trailers to 22', no hookups, piped water, flush toilets, fishing, trail to ocean, in Siuslaw NF, $10 to $18/night.

North of Florence 6 miles via US 101, then FSR 794 northwest 1.6 miles.

X) JESSIE M. HONEYMAN STATE PARK
382 campsites, 66 w/full hookups, 75 w/electricity, plus 240 tent units, mail reservations available, maximum site 55', picnic area, wheelchair access, showers, trailer waste disposal, boat launch, fishing, swimming, hiking trails, sand dunes, lakes, wild rhododendrons, $15 to $17/night.

South of Florence 3 miles on US 101.

Y) DRIFTWOOD II FS CAMP
70 units, trailers to 50', no hookups, piped water, flush toilets – wheelchair access, ocean fishing, hiking, ORV, in Siuslaw NF, pets okay, $10 to $18/night.

South of Florence 7 miles via US 101, FSR 1078 west 1.4 miles.

Z) SURFWOOD CAMPGROUND
163 campsites, 100 w/full hookups, 41 w/water & electricity, plus 22 tent units, reservation information - (503)271-4020, showers, laundry, groceries, swimming pool, playground, tennis, trailer waste disposal, stream, pets okay, $12 to $14/night.

Southwest of Reedsport 2 miles on US 101.

AA) WILLIAM M. TUGMAN STATE PARK
115 campsites w/electricity, maximum site to 50', picnic area, wheelchair access, showers, trailer waste disposal, boat launch, fishing, swimming, $14/night.

South of Reedsport 8 miles on US 101.

BB) LOON LAKE LODGE RESORT
100 campsites, 37 w/water & electricity, plus 78 w/no hookups, reservations - (503)599-2244, groceries, restaurant/lounge, lake, swimming, fishing, boat launch, boat rental, hiking, pets okay, $10 to $14/night.

Southeast of Reedsport. State 38 east 13 miles, then CR 3 south 8.2 miles.

CC) CHARLESTON MARINA & TRAVEL PARK
109 campsites w/full hookups, plus 10 tent units, reservation information - (503)888-9512, showers, laundry, trailer waste disposal, ocean access, river, fishing, boat launch, playground. pets okay, $10 to $14/night.

In Charleston. At west end of Charleston Bridge head north on Boat Basin Drive for 2 blocks, and turn east on Kingfisher Drive.

DD) BASTENDORFF BEACH COUNTY PARK
81 campsites, 56 w/water & electricity, plus 25 tent units, trailers to 70', showers, trailer waste disposal, flush toilets, playground, ocean access, fishing, pets okay, $11 to $13/night.

South of Charleston 2 miles via the Cape Arago Highway.

EE) SUNSET BAY STATE PARK
139 campsites, 29 w/full hookups, 35 w/water & electricity, 75 tent units, plus hiker/biker camp, maximum site 47', mail reservations available, picnic area, wheelchair access, showers, beach access, $4 to $17/night.

South of Charleston, on Sunset Bay.

FF) BULLARDS BEACH STATE PARK
192 campsites, 92 w/full hookups, 100 w/electricity, plus hiker/biker & horse camps, maximum site 64', picnic area, wheelchair access, showers, trailer waste disposal, boat launch, fishing, horse trails & facilities, ocean access, $4 to $17/night.

North of Bandon 1 mile on US 101.

GG) BANDON/PORT ORFORD KOA
74 campsites, 16 w/full hookups, 24 w/water & electricity, plus 34 tent units, reservations - (503)348-2358, showers, laundry, trailer waste disposal, playground, hiking, pets okay, $16 to $20/night.

South of Langlois 3 miles on US 101.

HH) CAPE BLANCO STATE PARK
58 campsites w/hookups for electricity, plus hiker/biker & horse camps, maximum site 70', picnic area, wheelchair access, showers, trailer waste disposal, fishing, ocean access, black sand beach, beachcombing, hiking, $4 to $16/night.

Northwest of Port Orford 4 miles on US 101, then follow signs west 5 miles.

II) HUMBUG MOUNTAIN STATE PARK
108 campsites, 30 w/full hookups, 78 tent units, plus hiker/ biker camp, maximum site 55', picnic area, wheelchair access, showers, trailer waste disposal, ocean access, hiking trail, $4 to $17/night.

South of Port Orford 6 miles on US 101.

JJ) ARIZONA BEACH CAMPGROUND
127 campsites, 11 w/full hookups, 85 w/water & electricity, plus 31 tent units, reservations - (503)332-6491, showers, laundry, groceries, trailer waste disposal, swimming, fishing, playfield, pets okay, $14 to $19/night.

North of Gold Beach 14 miles on US 101.

KK) HONEY BEAR CAMPGROUND

150 campsites, 55 w/full hookups, 18 w/water & electricity, plus 77 tent units, information - (503)247-2765, wheelchair access, showers, laundry, trailer waste disposal, swimming, fishing, playfield, playground, hiking, pets okay, $14 to $17/night.

North of Gold Beach 7 miles via US 101, then Ophir Road north 2 miles to campground.

LL) INDIAN CREEK RECREATION PARK

125 campsites, 100 w/full hookups, plus 25 tent units, reservation information - (503)247-7704, showers, laundry, river, fishing, playfield, wheelchair access, pets okay, $12 to $20/night.

East of Gold Beach. Leave US 101 at south end of Rogue River bridge, and go east .5 mile on Jerry's Flat Road.

MM) HARRIS BEACH STATE PARK

156 campsites, 34 w/full hookups, 53 w/electricity, plus 69 tent units, mail reservations available, maximum site 50', picnic area, wheelchair access, showers, trailer waste disposal, fishing, ocean access, hiking trails, $15 to $17/night.

North of Brookings 2 miles on US 101.

NN) BEACH FRONT RV PARK

184 campsites, 48 w/full hookups, 56 w/water & electricity, plus 75 w/out hookups, tents okay, reservations - (800)441-0856, showers, laundry, trailer waste disposal, river, swimming, fishing, boat launch, wheelchair access, $7 to $14/night.

In Brookings – take Lower Harbor Road to Benham Lane.

OO) DRIFTWOOD RV PARK

108 campsites, 100 w/full hookups, plus 8 w/water & electricity, no tents, reservations - (503)469-3213, showers, laundry, fishing, pets okay, $15 to $16/night.

South of Brookings. US 101 over Chetco River Bridge, to Lower Harbor Road, west .7 mile.

PP) CHETCO RV PARK

120 trailer sites w/full hookups - 80 are pull-thru sites, no tents, adults only, small pets okay, reservation information - (503)469-3863, showers, laundry, trailer waste disposal, $17/night.

South of Brookings 1 mile past Chetco River Bridge on US 101.

QQ) LOEB STATE PARK

53 campsites w/water & electricity, picnic area, flush toilets, showers, nature trail, swimming, fishing, rafting, $14/night.

Northeast of Brookings 8 miles on North Bank Road.

Camping
Vacation
#6

An Ice Age Vacation
in Eastern Washington

FROM THE AUTHOR'S JOURNAL . . .

There I was, standing at the edge of America's largest waterfall, and without the interpretive center and signs marking its significance I would never have seen it.

Today Dry Falls is just that, dry. But at one time the water rushed over it with enough force to be heard for a hundred miles.

Imagine, a waterfall 3.5 times wider and 2.5 times higher than Niagara Falls. One that appeared almost overnight. Nearly half of North America's glacial floodwaters had thundered through here during the final days of the Ice Age.

This is a trip to be remembered, not for its beauty, although the deserts of eastern Washington can be quite beautiful. This is a trip that will be remembered because it so vividly brings the Ice Age into the present.

After Dry Falls, I viewed the Grand Coulee landscape differently. Those weren't just chasms, valleys, and rocks that provided my eyes with a pleasant experience. They were part of a historic time that had, until then, been only a name given to an era I'd had to memorize for a grade school history test.

Notes from my first Ice Age vacation

AN ICE AGE VACATION
IN EASTERN WASHINGTON

Let your imagination carry you back 13,000 years. You are in eastern Washington, and the gently rolling hills are covered with a 200-foot deep blanket of windblown silt. The 15,000-square-mile area circling current day Odessa is a shallow lava bowl tipped so that its southwest rim is 2,000 feet lower than the northeast edge.

You are witnessing the end of the Ice Age. Massive glaciers have covered the land to the north for more than 750,000 years. They extend southward into the Okanogan, San Poil, Columbia, Colville, and Pend Oreille Valleys. Ice has damned the rivers, creating vast lakes and forcing the water to seek new paths.

Glacial Lake Missoula is the largest of all the Ice Age lakes. Its 600 cubic miles of water cover 3,000 square miles of northwest Montana. It is 2000 feet deep near the mammoth ice dam that holds it in the mountains.

Summer arrives and the rain begins to fall. This speeds the melting of winter snow and hastens the retreat of the glaciers' southernmost edges. The added water begins to push Lake Missoula over the top of the dam, and with a thundering crash the dam washes away. The lake empties in less than 48 hours.

As this mammoth wall of water travels, it destroys valley ice dams, adding more water to its volume. Surging into eastern Washington's giant lava bowl, it picks up speed at an alarming rate. The land is scraped bare, and giant slabs of rock are pulled from the earth. The rivers are 20 miles wide, up to 600 feet deep, and move at 45 miles per hour. Within two weeks, most of the water makes its way to the sea, leaving behind a drastically altered landscape.

Thousands of years later you can still see the course taken by that massive wall of water. Giant ripple marks, large deposits of foreign rocks and boulders, huge gravel bars, formidable river deltas, and isolated dry islands forever mark its path. The rolling hills and lush loess have been replaced by abrupt rock cliffs, oddly carved canyons, giant cataracts, and 200-foot-deep plunge pools.

Eastern Washington has long caught the interest of vacationers. They come to play in the waters of the Columbia, Snake and Spokane Rivers, most never knowing how this strange landscape was created. Someday, visitors will come just to view the channeled scablands carved by that destructive rush of water we now call the Spokane Flood. Today's visitors can enjoy it naturally, before signs mark every feature and souvenir shops dot the horizon.

Seeing the Ice Age Features
The **Odessa Visitor Center [1]** is an excellent place to begin your Ice Age vacation. Start with the short video showing how the scablands were formed, and pick up a free driving tour brochure. This will lead you to a number of close-in places where the flood's devastation is still visible.

Odessa is right in the center of the great flood's middle channel, on the **Crab Creek Floodway [2]**. This region is like no other part of Washington. It consists of a hodge-podge collection of dry canyons and water-ravaged craters. This land was once covered with great seas of lava. They came in floods, each covering the last, which gives the surrounding cliffs a variety of textures. Look closely, and you can easily see where the different flows of red hot lava begin and end.

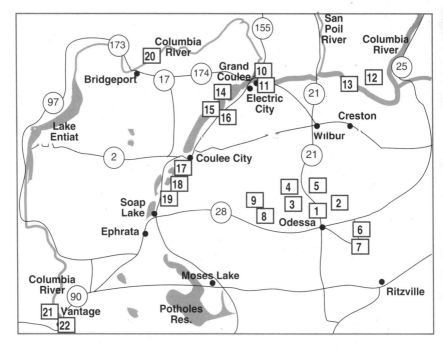

Ice Age Landscape Attractions

Take Lakeview Ranch Road three miles north of town, and you'll find 5,000 acres of Ice Age landscape to explore. This is **Lakeview Ranch [3]**, a rugged BLM property that also offers primitive campsites, pit toilets, drinking water, picnic tables, shade, horse and hiking trails, a horse-loading chute and corrals.

Lakeview is a good home base for extensive scabland exploration. Special ranch features include the serene Lake Creek Coulee, enormous Lakeview Ranch Crater, a maze of anastomosing channels, Waukesha Spring, and lots of desert rangeland.

There's also a wonderful collection of flood-ravaged volcano craters seven miles north of Odessa, at the junction of Highway 21 and Coffeepot Road. **Cache Crater [4]** is west of the highway; **Rock Rose, Hidden Crater, Wild Garden, Amphitheater and Cinnamon**

Roll [5] are all to the east. Each crater is different, but all show the effects of the flood on the ancient lava. Trails allow for close-up exploration, but keep your eyes peeled for rattlesnakes and porcupines.

Photo Courtesy of Odessa Economic Development Committee

You'll find more Ice Age features by heading east of Odessa 13 miles on Highway 28 to Lamona Road. This road will take you into the **Coal Creek Coulee [6]**. Its walls have a lot of small basalt caves that were created when the floodwater pulled out large chunks of rock.

Follow Lamona Road south 7 miles and you'll see Crab Creek. To the east, an upright columnade marks the bottom of the **Roza Flow [7]**. Head west on Laney Road to get back to Odessa. This route offers a good view of the floodway. Imagine this gorge filled to the top with bubbling lava, and again with ice-filled water.

More Ice Age scenery awaits you west of Odessa. Drive 10 miles to Irby Road and turn north. Leaving the highway, you are at first traveling on lava from the Roza flow, then between columns formed during the **Frenchman Springs Flows [8]**.

Reaching the floor of Crab Creek, you are looking at cliffs created by the region's most catastrophic eruptions, the **Grand Ronde Basalt Flows [9]**. Standing here, you have 4,000 feet of lava from more than 100 separate flows beneath your feet. During the great flood, the water here was 300 feet deep.

The soil to the north resembles the loess that covered this entire region prior to the flood. This area was an isolated island during the flood, circled by a swirling mass of muddy water that was filled with huge chunks of ice, house-sized rocks and uprooted trees.

The Grand Coulee
Follow Highways 21 and 174 north/northwest of Odessa to **Grand Coulee [10]**. This steep-walled chasm was created when the Ice Age Columbia River became blocked by glaciers, forcing it across the lava field to where it could carve a new channel. The Grand Coulee is 50 miles long and up to 900 feet deep.

At the **Grand Coulee Dam [11]** visitors' center you can see how North America's largest hydroelectric dam was built, examine some of the artifacts found here, get information on local recreation, pick up a tour map, and take a 30-minute tour of the dam.

On summer evenings the dam serves as a backdrop for a laser light show, one of the world's largest. It features 300-foot-high animated images, beautifully accompanied by music and narrative, lasting about 40 minutes. From Memorial Day weekend through July the show begins at 10:00 p.m., in August it starts a half-hour earlier, and in September at 8:30 p.m. To get a good seat, be sure to arrive an hour early.

Photo Courtesy of U.S. Dept. of Interior/Grand Coulee Project Office

The building of this dam also created Lake Roosevelt, and with it, more than 600 miles of recreational lakeshore. Managed as the **Coulee Dam National Recreation Area [12]**, these parklands provide public access to some beautiful high deserts, dense pine forests, a number of campgrounds and family parks.

Fishing on **Lake Roosevelt [13]** and nearby **Banks Lake [14]** is good year round. Bass, trout, kokanee, perch, crappie, whitefish, ling cod, sunfish, sturgeon and chinook salmon are all caught here.

Steamboat Rock State Park [15] is 8 miles south of Grand Coulee and centers on a flat-topped butte rising

1,000 feet above Banks Lake. The butte, Steamboat Rock, was once an island in the ancient Columbia River. A trail to the top provides a panoramic view of the landscape and access to 640 quiet acres.

The **Banks Lake Wildlife Refuge [16]** is located midway between Electric City and Coulee City. It provides a safe haven for at least 16 kinds of waterfowl, including western grebe, great blue heron and the common loon, plus about 40 species of dryland birds.

The Largest Waterfall on Earth

About 4 miles southwest of Coulee City, you'll find the most impressive of all the Ice Age Flood features, **Dry Falls [17]**. This was once the largest waterfall on earth. Water 300 feet deep raced over its rocky edge with such force that it shook the ground and created a roar that could have been heard 100 miles away.

At one time, this dry rim held a waterfall 3.5 times wider and 2.5 times higher than Niagara Falls. Nearly half of all the glacial floodwaters in North America thundered over this spot. Its 400 foot cliffs provide unshakeable testimony to one of the most spectacular geologic events on our planet.

The Dry Falls Visitor Center is only open from the middle of May to late September, between 10:00 a.m. and 6:00 p.m. Inside you can watch a video on Ice Age Floods, and see exhibits explaining the changes here during the last 20 million years.

Outside, a viewpoint overlooks the now empty falls. During the summer you'll often find a ranger there to point out this natural landmark's special features. Hiking trails too allow for closer inspection.

The Dry Falls area is part of **Sun Lakes State Park [18]**. Besides camping facilities, this 3,365-acre park offers 3 lakes, a tree shaded picnic grove, swimming beach and restrooms.

About 5 miles south of Sun Lakes State Park, along Highway 17, are the **Lake Lenore Caves [19]**. Created when melting glaciers forced chunks of basalt from the coulee walls, these tiny pocket caves are thought to have been used as temporary shelters by nomadic prehistoric hunters.

The summer temperature in eastern Washington is generally hot. However, between the **Columbia River [20]**, Lake Roosevelt, and other local lakes you'll find plenty of water to play in during your Ice Age vacation. To avoid sunstroke, do any strenuous hiking early in the day, and spend the afternoon inside, or around water.

A Petrified Forest

If your travels take you near the junction of I-90 and the Columbia River, on your way to or from your vacation, stop at Vantage for a look at the **Ginkgo Petrified Forest State Park [21]**. Once there, you can hike along a prehistoric lakebed where 20-million-year-old logs exist in petrified form.

This land was lush, with lots of trees and ferns, before volcanic eruptions created the Cascade Mountain Range. When the hot lava hit the swamp forest, it formed molten rock pillows. Because the water smothered the heat, the plant life was not completely consumed. Instead, more than 200 different species of trees were petrified. The most unusual is the Ginkgo tree, a species that has been around for around 250 million years.

The Native Americans who lived in this area used the petrified wood to make arrowheads and trinkets. They also created more than 300 petroglyphs near the current park site. Most were buried under **Wanapum Reservoir [22]**, but a few have been put on display at the park.

Stop at the Interpretive Center first, before following one of the two short hiking trails. The center offers a terrific slide show that explains the evolution of this area, as well as samples of the hundreds of different kinds of petrified wood found here. Budget problems have hit this site pretty hard, but you'll usually find the center open from mid-June to mid-September, between 10:00 a.m. and 6:00 p.m., Wednesday thru Sunday.

The Ginkgo Petrified Forest State Park also has a public swimming beach, boat launch and picnic facilities, down by the Columbia River.

For Additional Information
The Odessa Visitor Information Center offers an easy-to-follow driving tour brochure of the Ice Age features surrounding this small town. It provides a good basis for in-depth explorations. For further information on other attractions, call the numbers listed below.

Odessa Visitor Information .... (509) 982-2232

Coulee Dam Visitors' Center .... (509) 633-9503

Coulee Dam Recreation Area .... (509) 633-9441

Dry Falls Visitor Center .... (509) 632-5214

Sun Lakes State Park .... (509) 632-5583

Ginkgo Petrified Forest State Park ...... (509) 856-2700

Ice Age Area Campgrounds

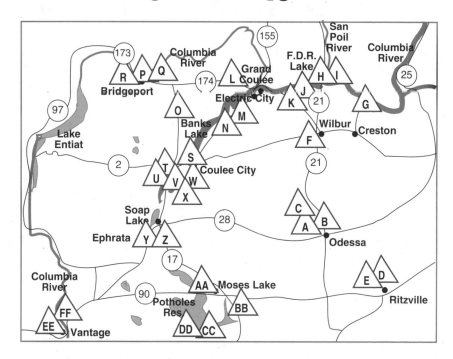

A) ODESSA GOLF COURSE & RV PARK
12 campsites w/water & electricity, reservations - (509)982-0093, on golf course – golfers stay for free, pets okay, $3 to $7/night.

At west end of Odessa.

B) ODESSA TOURIST PARK
Campsite area in city park - no fee, flush toilets, drinking water.

In Odessa, at the corner of 1st Avenue and Second Street.

C) LAKEVIEW BLM RANCH
Large primitive camp area - no fee, 8,000 acre ranch, chemical toilets, drinking water, hiking, bird watching, horse corrals and loading chute, no off-road vehicles.

Located 3 miles north of Odessa via Highway 21.

D) COTTAGE RV PARK & MOTEL
19 campsites w/full hookups, no tents, showers, laundry, information - (509)659-0721, trailer waste disposal, $12/night.

In Ritzville, at city center.

118

E) BEST WESTERN HERITAGE INN & RV PARK
30 campsites w/full hookups, plus 10 tent sites, information - (509)659-1007, wheelchair access, showers, laundry, swimming pool, therapy pool, $18/night.

Leave I-90 on exit #221, located along frontage road.

F) BELLS TRAILER PARK
30 trailer sites w/full hookups, reservations - (509)647-5888, showers, laundry, picnic area, $12/night.

Located in Wilbur, at the east end of town; one block off US 2.

G) HAWK CREEK CDRA CAMPGROUND
28 campsites, trailers okay, no hookups, well water, lake, fishing, boat launch & dock, pets okay, $10/night.

Take US 2 east of Wilbur to Creston, then go north 17 miles.

H) THE RIVER RUE RV PARK
61 units, 19 w/full hookups, 21 w/water & electricity, plus 21 tent sites, reservations - (509)647-2647, wheelchair access, showers, playground, trailer waste disposal, $10 to $15/night.

North of Wilbur 14 miles on State 21.

I) KELLER FERRY CDRA CAMPGROUND
55 campsites, trailers okay, no hookups, picnic area, trailer & boat waste disposal, boat ramp & dock, swimming, $10/night.

North of Wilbur on State 21 approximately 14 miles.

J) SPRING CANYON CDRA CAMP
97 campsites, trailers okay, no hookups, drinking water, picnic area, handicap access, trailer & boat waste disposal, boat dock & ramp, swimming, pets okay, $10/night.

Take State 174 southeast of Grand Coulee 5 miles to campground road and follow 1.1 miles north.

K) LAKEVIEW TERRACE RV PARK
25 trailer sites w/full hookups, information - (509)633-2169, showers, laundry, playfield, playground, $8.50 to $12/night.

Southeast of Grand Coulee 3 miles on State 174.

L) CURLY'S CAMPGROUND
22 campsites, 16 w/full hookups, plus 6 tent units, information - (509)633-0750, showers, $9 to $13/night.

Northwest of Grand Coulee 2 miles on State 174.

M) COULEE PLAYLAND RESORT & RV PARK
65 campsites, 40 w/full hookups, 13 w/water & electricity, plus

12 tent sites, information - (509)633-2671, showers, laundry, on Banks Lake, playground, trailer waste disposal, swimming, fishing, boat launch, boat rental, $13 to $17/night.

Take State 155 west of Grand Coulee1.0 mile.

N) STEAMBOAT ROCK STATE PARK
100 campsites w/full hookups, tents okay, wheelchair access, on Banks Lake, boat launch, fishing, water skiing, scuba diving, trailer waste disposal, pets okay, $10 to $16/night.

Take State 155 7.2 miles southwest of Grand Coulee, to campground road.

O) BLUE LAKE RESORT
75 campsites, 23 w/full hookups, 33 w/water & electricity, plus 19 tent units, information - (509)632-5364, showers, groceries, tackle store, playfield, playground, lake, swimming, fishing, boat launch & rental, $9.50 to $11.50/night.

US 2 west of Coulee City 2 miles, then State 17 south 10 miles.

P) WATERFRONT MARINA CITY CAMPGROUND
34 trailer sites w/water & electricity, plus 14 w/no hookups, showers, picnic area, information – (509)686-7231, playground, trailer waste disposal, river fishing, pets okay, $11 to $16/night.

In Bridgeport, at Columbia Avenue & 7th Street.

Q) BRIDGEPORT STATE PARK
34 units, 20 w/water & electricity, plus 14 tent sites, trailers to 45', wheelchair accessible, on Lake Rufus Woods, trailer waste disposal, boat launch, fishing, $10 to $15/night.

At Bridgeport take State 173 to State 17, then go north 1.5 miles.

R) ROCK GARDEN RV PARK
40 campsites, 12 w/full hookups, 8 w/water & electricity, plus lots of tent sites, information - (509)686-5343, showers, laundry, trailer waste disposal, river, fishing, playground, $5 to $13/night.

Located northwest of Bridgeport 2.5 miles via State 173.

S) COULEE CITY PARK
140 campsites, 34 w/full hookups, plus 106 tent units, trailers to 24', information - (509)632-5331, showers, playground, trailer waste disposal, lake swimming, fishing, boat launch, pets okay, $8 to $10/night.

In Coulee City, at northern edge of town.

T) SUN LAKES STATE PARK
193 units, 18 w/full hookups, no fire pits, wheelchair access,

trailer waste disposal, boat & horse rental, boat launch, fishing, swimming, horse trails, pets okay, $15 to $16/night.

US 2 west of Coulee City 2 miles, then State 17 south 5 miles.

U) SUN LAKES PARK RESORT
110 trailer sites w/full hookups, tents okay, no fire pits, information - (509)632-5291, showers, laundry, groceries, trailer waste disposal, swimming pool, playfield, lake, fishing, boat launch & rental, golf & mini golf, hiking, $15 to $16/night.

US 2 west of Coulee City 2 miles, then State 17 south 7 miles.

V) LAURENTS SUN VILLAGE RESORT
100 units, 56 w/full hookups, 40 w/water & electricity, plus 4 tent sites, information - (509)632-5664, pull-thrus, showers, laundry, rec room, lake, boat rentals/dock & launch, water skiing, playground, fishing, hiking, picnic area, $12 to $15/night.

US 2 west of Coulee City 2 miles, State 17 south 8 miles, and State Park Road east 1 mile to resort.

W) COULEE LODGE RESORT
45 units, 22 w/full hookups, 11 w/water & electricity, plus 12 tent sites, information - (509)632-5565, wheelchair access, showers, laundry, trailer waste disposal, lake, swimming, fishing, boat launch & rental, $10 to $13.50/night.

US 2 west of Coulee City 2 miles, then State 17 south 8 miles.

X) SUN VILLAGE RESORT
115 campsites, 95 w/full hookups, plus 20 w/water & electricity, information - (509)632-5664, showers, laundry, groceries, playground, trailer waste disposal, lake, swimming, fishing, boat launch & rental, $12 to $15/night.

US 2 west of Coulee City 2 miles, then State 17 south 8 miles.

Y) OASIS PARK
69 campsites, 31 w/full hookups, 38 w/water & electricity, plus big tent area, information - (509)754-5102, wheelchair access, showers, laundry, covered picnic area, pool, golf & mini golf, playfield, trailer waste disposal, swimming, fishing, hiking, pets okay, $8.50 to $12/night.

Located in Ephrata.

Z) SOAP LAKES SMOKIAM CITY CAMPGROUND
52 campsites w/full hookups, tents okay, showers, groceries, laundry, trailer waste disposal, playground, lake swimming, fishing, Soap Lake mud baths, pets okay, $7 to $10/night.

Northwest of Moses Lake 26 miles via State 17.

AA) BIG SUN RESORT & RV PARK

50 campsites w/full hookups, plus 10 tent sites, information - (509)765-8294, wheelchair access, showers, laundry, playground, on Moses Lake, boat launch & rental, $10 to $15/night.

In Moses Lake. Leave I-90 at exit #176 and take Broadway north .5 mile, campground is west, at 2300 W. Marina Drive.

BB) WILLOWS TRAILER VILLAGE

64 campsites, 38 w/full hookups, 8 w/water & electricity, plus large tent area, information - (509)765-7531, showers, laundry, playfield, trailer waste disposal, pets okay, $10 to $15/night.

Take State 17 south of I-90 2 miles, and CR M southeast .3 mile.

CC) MAR DON RESORT

350 campsites, 160 w/full hookups, 55 w/water & electricity, 135 w/out hookups, plus beach tent area, information - (509)765-5061, showers, playground, large fish supply & grocery store, on Potholes Reservoir, marina, boat moorage, fishing dock, boat launch, swimming beach, hiking, $12 to $17/night.

Take State 17 south of I-5 10 miles, then Potholes Reservoir Road west 8 miles.

DD) POTHOLES STATE PARK

126 units, 60 w/full hookups, plus 66 tent sites, wheelchair accessible trails, trailer waste disposal, on Potholes Reservoir, boat launch, fishing, water skiing, pets okay, $10 to $15/night.

Take State 17 south of I-5 10 miles, then Potholes Reservoir Road west 13 miles.

EE) VANTAGE KOA

150 campsites, 100 w/full hookups - 14 pull-thrus, plus 36 tent units, information - (509)856-2230, showers, laundry, groceries, rec room, playground, swimming pool, therapy pool, trailer waste disposal, on Columbia River, swimming, fishing, pets okay, $15 to $20/night.

In Vantage. Located 2 blocks north of I-90 exit #136.

FF) GINKGO/WANAPUM STATE PARK

50 sites w/full hookups, Ginkgo Petrified Forest, boat launch, fishing, beach access, trail, pets okay, $15/night.

North of Vantage. Take I-90 east 1 mile to park exit.

Camping
Vacation
#7

The Best of the
Columbia River Gorge

Having spent most of my life in the Portland area, I've explored the Columbia River Gorge pretty thoroughly.

Visitors always got the standard waterfall tour, and if they were the kind of people who appreciate art they were taken to Maryhill and Stonehenge. Whenever I was looking for a close-in hike, I always knew I could find some place special by heading up the gorge.

Now it's a national treasure. There are more out-of-state license plates than local, and visiting windsurfers have overrun its once quiet beaches. But the Columbia River Gorge still retains some of the special qualities that have always brought me here, I just have to look a little harder.

Since most Gorge visitors are just driving through, or are there only to ride the wind and water, those of us who are looking for a less crowded experience only have to travel inland to get away from most of the congestion.

Off-season travel is also a good way to avoid the vacationing masses. The waterfalls are at their best in the spring, and Oneonta Gorge has very few visitors in the fall. And when it comes to hiking, I've found that any trail longer than four miles is beyond the energy of most casual visitors, any time of the year.

Thoughts on avoiding the crowds that fame as a National Recreation Area has brought to the Columbia River Gorge

THE BEST OF THE
COLUMBIA RIVER GORGE

The **Columbia River Gorge National Scenic Area [1]** begins 16 miles east of Portland, and includes land on both sides of the river. It preserves a lush, water-filled canyon nature has cut through the Cascade Mountains, and is lined with breathtaking waterfalls, impressive forests and sheer basalt cliffs.

Because of its proximity to Portland and its national recreational status, the gorge is sometimes overrun with people. But even those seeking solitude can find happiness, if they just spend a little time researching the area.

Three bridges span the Columbia River within the scenic area, providing easy access to attractions on both sides. They are found at Oregon's Cascade Locks, Hood River, and The Dalles.

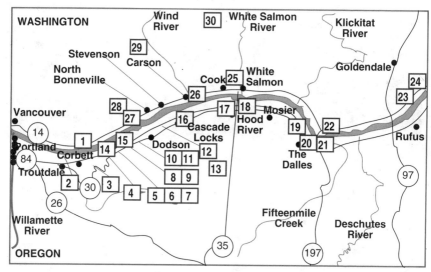

Columbia River Gorge Attractions

The **Columbia River Scenic Highway [2]** stretches between Troutdale and The Dalles, just south of I-84. Built between 1913 and 1925, it originally covered 83 miles, traveling over creeks and rivers, around foothills, and through towering basalt cliffs. This colossal endeavor was constructed entirely by hand. Nearly 60 miles of the original route is maintained, providing travelers with spectacular views, trail access, and the opportunity to view several waterfalls.

Following this highway, most visitors make their first stop after 5 miles, at **Crown Point Vista House [3]**. Built in 1918, this historic stone structure is perched high above the river and provides an expansive view.

An Abundance of Waterfalls
Heading east, you'll travel past nine waterfalls. The first, 224' **Latourelle Falls [4]**, was originally called Was-ke-wa by the region's Native Americans. According to legend, the falls were formed when the creator, Speelyie, threw one of his wives over the mountains. Her hair is represented by the water. Today it carries the name of a pioneer family.

At **Sheppard's Dell [5]**, Young's Creek drops into a quiet cove. It can be viewed from the bridge, or you can take the stairs down for a closer look. Logging has destroyed most of **Bridal Veil Falls' [6]** power and beauty. You'll find what's left of it beneath the bridge at the village of Bridal Veil.

Mist Falls [7] is splendid, and the 242' **Wahkeena Falls [8]** is actually a series of waterfalls. Wah-ke-nah is an Indian word meaning "most beautiful", and this spot is appropriately named. The upper falls are known as Little Fairy and Ghost Falls.

Next, you'll come to the gorge's most famous feature, **Multnomah Falls [9]**. At 620', it is the United States' second highest waterfall and accessible from both the scenic highway and I-84. It's a short stroll to the bottom of the falls, and an easy hike to the bridge viewpoint. If you've got the energy, hike all the way to the top for a panoramic view.

Be sure to check out the historic Multnomah Falls Lodge. Its walls are said to contain samples of every kind of rock found within the Columbia River Gorge.

Follow Highway 30 east of Multnomah Falls 25 miles to explore **Oneonta Gorge [10]**. This picturesque

crevice was created by an ancient earthquake. Follow the creek back and you'll find a lovely, secluded waterfall. This little treasure is reached by wading the creek. In the late summer, when the water is low, it's a wonderful family adventure. It doesn't take long, and is a great way to beat the heat.

Horsetail Falls [11] is just a short distance beyond Oneonta Gorge. One look at this 208' cascade is all you need to understand why it was so named. **Elowah Falls [12]** drops 289' at McCord Creek, and dozens of lesser known waterfalls are found in the hills.

Hiking Trails and Windsurfing Beaches

The **Mt. Hood National Forest [13]** covers a vast area south of the river, and provides hikers with a wealth of trails. The gorge section alone has more than 150 miles of trails. These will lead you off the beaten path, rewarding your efforts with unsurpassable views and a chance to enjoy those hidden waterfalls.

Stop at the forest service office in Troutdale for personal help in finding the right trail. Beginners should ask about the Latourelle Falls, Multnomah-Wahkeena Loop, and Elowah Falls Trails. Experienced hikers will enjoy the Ruckel Creek Trails and the one up Nick Eaton Ridge. If you really want a workout, check out the Gorton Creek and Mt. Defiance Trails.

Windsurfing is very popular in the gorge. In fact, Hood River is considered the windsurfing capital of the Northwest. **Rooster Rock State Park [14]**, **Dalton Point [15]** and **Cascade Locks Park [16]** are hot, as is the **Hood River Marina [17]**, **Koberg Beach [18]** and **Mayer State Park [19]**. The Dalles' **Riverfront Park [20]** is popular with beginners.

You can take a free train ride at **The Dalles Dam [21]**. It operates May thru September, every half hour from 10:00 a.m. to 5:00 p.m. At the end of the ride, you can watch as fish make their way up the fish ladders, tour the powerhouse, see the massive generators, and learn how the river is used to create power.

Before the dam's construction, the rock cliffs here contained more than 400 ancient petroglyphs and pictographs. A few were removed before the rising waters buried them and are on display at the dam.

The Washington Shore
Cross the river at The Dalles and head east on Highway 14. You'll find a few pictographs among the rocks at **Horsethief Lake State Park [22]**, 2 miles east of Highway 14's junction with Highway 197. Park by the west boat ramp and take the path on the right to view this ancient artwork. A picnic area is also available at the park.

Continue east a short distance on Highway 14 for an opportunity to tour Eastern Washington's finest art museum. The **Maryhill Art Museum [23]** is housed in a stately old mansion, surrounded by miles of sparsely populated desert.

Maryhill's displays include Rodin sculptures, colorful Russian icons, ornate Romanian furnishings, Native American art and artifacts, Galle art glass and other rare treats. You'll also find one-of-a-kind collections, including the elegantly dressed *Theatre de la Mode* miniature Parisian fashion mannequins and over 100 antique chess sets. The museum is open from March 15th to November 15th, 9:00 a.m. to 5:00 p.m., and is a real bargain at $4.00 for adults, $1.50 for kids.

Just east of the museum you can see a full-size replica of England's Stonehenge. Perched on a bluff, overlooking the Columbia, this **Stonehenge [24]** was built in remembrance of local residents killed during World War I. It was the United States' first WWI memorial. At the time of construction, the original Stonehenge was thought to have been a sacrificial site, a fact the builder found to be a fitting accolade to war.

Heading back along the Washington shore, Highway 14 follows much of the route taken by Lewis and Clark during their famous expedition.

Although you can visit year round, September is the best time to see the large chinook salmon at **Spring Creek Fish Hatchery [25]**. They rear about 17 million fingerlings here each year. You can visit daily between

7:30 a.m. and 4:00 p.m. To get there, leave Highway 14 about 2 miles west of White Salmon, and follow the signs. It's less than a mile.

Windsurfers frequent **Home Valley Park [26]** as well as the public beaches around Stevenson and North Bonneville. The waters west of Highway 97 are also popular. Summer winds here generally blow at 20 to 30 mph, and a variety of conditions can be found. Even if you don't ride the waves, it's fun to watch.

Beacon Rock [27] is hard to miss, on the shore of the Columbia River west of Stevenson. A steep trail winds upward 900 feet, providing hikers with a birds-eye view of the gorge. The trail is not difficult, but it is steep, so you'll need to wear good shoes and allow plenty of time. The view is definitely worth the effort.

If you've got any energy left after climbing up and down Beacon Rock, cross the highway to Beacon Rock State Park and take the **Hamilton Mountain Trail [28]**. It will lead you over Rodney and Hardy Falls.

Exploring the Gifford Pinchot National Forest
Two of the Gifford Pinchot National Forest's prettiest districts are found just north of the Columbia River. **Wind River Valley [29]**, north of Carson, and the **Trout Lake Area [30]** are both fun to explore.

In the Wind River district, the Paradise Trail will lead you through old growth conifers for a beautiful view of the upper valley. The Falls Creek Trail has a couple of nice waterfalls, and the Lower Falls Creek Trail takes you over the water on a log-stringer bridge. The Siouxon and Chinook Trails also lead to waterfalls.

Stop at the Wind River ranger's office in Carson for directions. Or better yet, contact the Gifford Pinchot National Forest headquarters when planning your trip, for maps and information.

The Trout Lake area is reached via Highway 141, west of White Salmon. Deadhorse, Dry Creek, Cheese, and Ice Caves are in this district, along with numerous hiking trails and berry fields. The Mt. Adams ranger station, in Trout Lake, is the best place to find out more about the caves and which trails fit your skills and schedule.

For Additional Information
The following agencies can provide you with detailed maps and information on Columbia River Gorge attractions. Request anything they have about the area, and you'll discover lots of out-of-the way sights that won't be too crowded. The Oregon State Parks department, for example, has a wonderful brochure showing lots of gorge trails.

Columbia River Gorge
  National Scenic Area ....(503) 386-2333

Oregon State Parks .... (800) 452-5687
  If calling from Portland 731-3411

Washington State Parks .... (206) 753-2027

Mt. Hood National Forest .... (503) 666-0771

Gifford Pinchot National Forest .... (206) 750-5000

Maryhill Art Museum .... (509) 773-3733

Columbia River Gorge Campgrounds

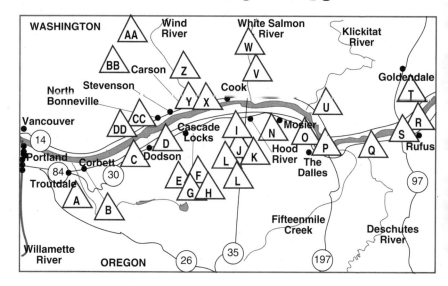

OREGON CAMPGROUNDS

A) OXBOW COUNTY PARK
45 campsites, trailers to 30', no hookups, pit toilets, fire pits, drinking water, river, fishing, boat launch, playfield, playground, wheelchair access, hiking, no pets, $9/night – 5 day max. stay.

East of Portland 8 miles on Division Street.

B) CROWN POINT RV PARK
20 trailer sites w/full hookups, plus a few tent sites, information - (503)695-5207, showers, laundry, trailer waste disposal, pets okay, $12 to $17/night.

East of Corbett .2 mile, on US 30, near milepost #9.

C) AINSWORTH STATE PARK
45 campsites w/full hookups, maximum site 60', picnic area, showers, trailer waste disposal, hiking, access to Columbia Gorge Trail, $15/night.

Located just west of where US 30's scenic route merges with I-84.

D) FISHERY - COVERTS LANDING
15 campsites w/electricity, tents okay, reservations - (503)374-8577, showers, wheelchair access, trailer waste disposal, gasoline, boat launch, boat moorage, fishing, $8 to $10/night.

Take exit #35 off I-84 at Dodson and follow signs to campground.

E) EAGLE CREEK FS CAMP
19 units, trailers to 22', flush toilets, wheelchair access, creek, fishing, hiking, bicycling, in Mt. Hood NF, pets okay, $8/night.

Leave I-84 4.5 miles west of Cascade Locks, go east on I-84 for 2 miles, then follow FSR 240 southeast .1 mile to campground.

F) CASCADE LOCKS MARINE PARK
38 campsites, no hookups, information - (503)374-8619, showers, trailer waste disposal, river, fishing, boat launch, playground, wheelchair access, wind surfing, $8/night.

In Cascade Locks, 3 blocks north of Cascade Locks exit off I-84.

G) BRIDGE OF THE GODS RV PARK
15 sites w/full hookups, no tents, reservations - (503)374-8628, showers, laundry, tv hookup, fishing, $15/night.

In Cascade Locks, on US 30, right before the bridge.

H) CASCADE LOCKS KOA
78 campsites, 40 w/full hookups, plus 38 w/water & electricity, information - (503)374-8668, showers, laundry, playground, pool, trailer waste disposal, pets okay, $15 to $19/night.

At east end of Cascade Locks, take Forest Lane southeast 1 mile.

I) VIENTO STATE PARK
75 campsites, 58 w/electricity, plus 17 tent units, maximum site 30', picnic area, showers, stream, hiking, $13 to $14/night.

West of Hood River 8 miles on I-84.

J) TUCKER COUNTY PARK
69 campsites, 13 w/water & electricity, plus 56 tent sites, reservations - (503)386-6323, showers, playfield & playground, picnic shelter, pets okay, $12 to $14/night.

South of Hood River 6 miles on Tucker Road.

K) ROUTSON COUNTY PARK
20 tent sites, reservations - (503)386-6323, flush toilets, stream, fishing, pets okay, $5/night.

South of Hood River on State 35 7 miles.

L) KINGSLEY FS CAMP
11 tent sites, lake water, pit toilets, lake, fishing, in Mt. Hood NF, pets okay, no fee.

South of Hood River, take FSR N20 for 12 miles to campground.

M) TOLL BRIDGE COUNTY PARK
85 campsites, 45 w/full hookups, 45 w/water & electricity, plus 20 tent sites, showers, wheelchair access, trailer waste disposal,

information - (503)386-6323, playfield, playground, hiking, river, fishing, pets okay, $12 to $14/night.

South of Hood River 18 miles on State 35.

N) AMERICAN ADVENTURE
350 campsites, 250 w/water & electricity, plus 100 tent sites, information - (503)478-3750, showers, picnic area, laundry, play area, wheelchair access, trailer waste disposal, pond fishing, swimming, hiking, spa, $14 to $18/night.

In Mosier, at 2350 Carroll Road.

O) MEMALOOSE STATE PARK
110 campsites, 43 w/full hookups, plus 67 tent units, maximum site 60', wheelchair access, showers, trailer waste disposal, $$-$15 to $17/night.

West of The Dalles 11 miles via I-84, only accessible westbound.

P) LONE PINE RV PARK
22 trailer sites w/full hookups, no tents, information - (503)296-9133, showers, laundry, river, fishing, playground, $20/night.

In The Dalles, near the north end of I-84's exit #87 overpass.

Q) DESCHUTES RIVER STATE PARK
34 primitive campsites, trailers to 30', fishing, hiking trails, $9/night.

East of The Dalles 17 miles via I-84.

R) LEPAGE PARK
20 campsites area, showers, trailer waste disposal, on John Day River, swimming area, fishing, boat launch, pets okay, no fee.

Take I-84 east of Rufus 4 miles and follow the signs.

S) BOB'S BUDGET RV & TRAILER PARK
26 trailer sites w/full hookups, plus 10 tent sites, wheelchair accessible, pull thrus to 60', reservations - (503)739-2829, showers, laundry, pets okay, $10 to $15/night.

Rufus exit #109 to Old Highway 30, then west .5 mile to Wallace Street, and .2 mile south.

WASHINGTON CAMPGROUNDS
T) MARYHILL STATE PARK
53 sites, 50 w/full hookups, community kitchen, wheelchair access, trailer waste disposal, on Columbia River, boat launch, fishing, swimming, wind surfing, water skiing, $10 to $16/night.

Take State 14 east of it junction with US 97 for 2 miles.

U) HORSETHIEF LAKE STATE PARK

12 units, some trailers - no hookups, trailer waste disposal, boat launches to Columbia River & Horsethief Lake, scuba diving area, fishing, pets okay, $10/night.

Take State 14 west of its junction with US 97 for 18 miles.

V) MOSS CREEK FS CAMP

18 units, trailers okay – no hookups, piped water, on river, wheelchair access, fishing, in Gifford Pinchot NF, $5/night.

North of Cook 8 miles on County Road 18.

W) OKLAHOMA FS CAMP

23 units, trailers to 22', no hookups, well, on Little White Salmon River, wheelchair access, fishing, in Gifford Pinchot NF, $6/night.

North of Cook 14.4 miles on County Road 18.

X) HOME VALLEY PARK

23 units, tents okay, showers, picnic area, wheelchair access, on Columbia River, swimming, fishing, windsurfing, $11/night.

Located just east of Carson, on State 14.

Y) CARSON HOT SPRINGS

25 units, 14 w/full hookups, plus 11 tent sites, reservations - (509)427-8292, showers, hot springs, therapy baths, picnic area, handicap access, trailer waste disposal, fishing, hiking, $4.50 to $12.50/night.

In Carson. At flashing yellow light go up hill past 4 way stop and golf course. Take an immediate left and go down the hill to resort.

Z) PANTHER CREEK FS CAMP

32 units, no hookups, trailers to 25', well, stream, fishing, hiking, horse trails & ramp, in Gifford Pinchot NF, $9 to $16/night.

Take County Road 92135 northwest of Carson 9 miles, then FSR 6517 east 1.5 miles, and FSR 65 south .1 mile to camp.

AA) PARADISE CREEK FS CAMP

42 units, no hookups, trailers to 25', well, river, wheelchair access, fishing, hiking, in Gifford Pinchot NF, $9 to $16/night.

Take County Road 92135 northwest of Carson 13.8 miles, then FSR 30 north 6.3 miles.

BB) BEAVER FS CAMP

27 units, trailers to 25', no hookups, flush toilets, wheelchair access, swimming, hiking, fishing, near Trapper Creek Wilderness Area, in Gifford Pinchot NF, $9 to $16/night.

Northwest of Carson 12.2 miles on County Road 30.

CC) LEWIS & CLARK CAMPGROUND/RV PARK

70 units, 20 w/full hookups, 40 w/water & electricity, plus 10 tent sites, information - (509)427-5559, showers, laundry, rec room, trailer waste disposal, river, fishing, hiking, 9 hole golf course next door to park, $13/night.

Head west of Carson on State 14 to milepost #37. Park is located about 1 mile west of North Bonneville, on Evergreen Drive.

DD) BEACON ROCK STATE PARK

33 units, no hookups, community kitchen & picnic shelter, wheelchair access, trailer waste facility, on Columbia River, boat launch, fishing, trail to the top of Beacon Rock, pets okay, $10/night.

West of North Bonneville 6 miles on State 14.

INDEX

140

ORDER COUPON

Please send:

___Unforgettable Pacific Northwest Camping
    Vacations – **Volume 1** @ $10.95 ea.   _____

___The Best Free Historic Attractions in OR/WA;
    Pacific Northwest Freebies Vol. 1 @ $10.95 ea. _____

___A Camper's Guide to OR/WA @ $12.95 ea.   _____

___Free Campgrounds of WA /OR @ $8.95 ea.   _____

___The Northwest Golfer @ $12.95 ea.   _____

                              Shipping   __2.00__

                    TOTAL ENCLOSED   _____

Name _____

Address _____

City/State/Zip Code _____

Send this order coupon to Ki² Enterprises, P.O. Box 186,
Willamina, Oregon 97396

✂--✂

Please send:

___Unforgettable Pacific Northwest Camping
    Vacations – **Volume 1** @ $10.95 ea.   _____

___The Best Free Historic Attractions in OR/WA;
    Pacific Northwest Freebies Vol. 1 @ $10.95 ea. _____

___A Camper's Guide to OR/WA @ $12.95 ea.   _____

___Free Campgrounds of WA /OR @ $8.95 ea.   _____

___The Northwest Golfer @ $12.95 ea.   _____

                              Shipping   __2.00__

                    TOTAL ENCLOSED   _____

Name _____

Address _____

City/State/Zip Code _____

Send this order coupon to Ki² Enterprises, P.O. Box 186,
Willamina, Oregon 97396

ABOUT THE AUTHOR

KiKi Canniff is a Pacific Northwest writer who specializes in books about Oregon & Washington. She is the Portland Oregonian's campground columnist, and an avid camper. KiKi also enjoys hiking, travel, history, nature, and exploring Pacific Northwest backroads.